THE WOLF THAT NEVER SLEEPS

THE WOLF THAT NEVER SLEEPS

A Story of Baden-Powell

by

MARGUERITE DE BEAUMONT

THE MODERN ST. GEORGE
Sketch by the Chief Scout

The Girl Guides Association
17–19 Buckingham Palace Road
London SW1W 0PT

First published November 1944
First paperback edition 1983
Reprinted 1984
Reprinted 1991

TO
JOHN CHANDLER

Printed and bound in the United Kingdom by
Staples Printers Rochester Limited,
Love Lane, Rochester, Kent.

CONTENTS

FOREWORD

It is not easy for me to write a Foreword to a book about my husband.

During his lifetime I shared him with so many millions of others, chiefly the boys and girls who belong to our Movement, and all of whom he cared about so much.

Now that he is no longer here on this earth with us, I feel that I must still continue to share him.

For me—naturally—thoughts of him are continuously in my mind, and memories will never grow dim.

But to those who never knew him in person, thoughts of him, and the realisation of what he was and what he did, needs must come through hearsay; and the understanding of him and of his life and work will come to them through the stories that are passed on to them by their parents, their Guide Captains and their Scoutmasters.

This book is written by someone who knew this great leader of youth when she was herself a child, and before the founding of the Boy Scouts and Girl Guides.

Then he was known to the world as "B.-P. of Mafeking." She gave him her young admiration and a glowing hero-worship, because of the name that he had made for himself as a soldier.

She talked with him in those early days, and he talked with her, because he loved to talk with children and delighted in their response to his stories and over the way their enthusiasm was kindled and their imagination fired.

The author of this book became a Scout, calling herself a "Girl Scout", at an age when no up-to-date Scoutmaster would have dared to enrol her! And then, when

Guides were started, she transferred to them with the same enthusiasm that she had shown for Scouting.

Because of this early friendship, and remembering her own childhood, she has written of "B.-P." as the Boy, Soldier, Scout, and Man, for she visualises him as all these.

The Boy? Yes, because the enthusiasms and the simplicity of the child remained with him until the end, harnessed to the mature brilliance of the Soldier and the Man.

I am so glad that this book has been written, and by one so well qualified to do so. I trust that it will be widely read, for not only will it help to keep his memory alive, but it will show to succeeding generations of boys and girls the great humanity of the man who loved his fellow men and women and was loved by them in return.

Olave Baden-Powell

HAMPTON COURT PALACE
November, 1944

HOW THIS STORY CAME TO BE WRITTEN

I LITTLE THOUGHT, years ago when I was a Girl Scout, that I should ever write a story about Baden-Powell. But so many girls and boys have asked me to tell them about him that I think they may like to have a story in writing. Other people, who know much more about making books than I do, have already written about the Chief Scout, but what I have tried to do in this story is to tell you what I know about him from my own experience, because I had the privilege of being one of his friends. All the small anecdotes in this story were told me by the Chief himself, and as I thought back to the days when I used to see him fairly often, I imagined the whole of his life as a splendid race run by a good and well-trained sportsman, and, of course, I imagined him as winning the race, which he undoubtedly did. So when I was thinking of a title for this story I decided to call it "The Straight Race—a Story of Baden-Powell". But things don't always work out just as you think they will, and one day as I was writing the story, my nephew came home from school and asked me what I was doing. I told him, and he said at once, "What are you going to call it?" So I read him one or two bits that I had written, and before telling him the title I had chosen I asked him what he would have called it. I did this because he was a youngster, like you are, and "all youngsters" (to quote the Chief) "are much of a muchness". He answered at once without hesitating: "I think that story should be called 'The Wolf that Never Sleeps'." So, as I thought that he was quite right and that other schoolboys and girls would probably agree with him, I decided to take his advice.

It was the wise people who decide about books and the publishing of them at Girl Guide Headquarters in London who asked me to write this story, and I should like to thank many of them who have given me encouragement and help with it. I also want to thank a Scout friend of the Chief's and of mine for the help he has given me.

Last, but not least, the Chief Guide has contributed to this story by writing the Foreword, and that, as you will realise, is a great honour, and I am grateful to her in consequence.

I think it may interest you to know that I am a Scoutmaster as well as a Guider, and that it is to my Scout Troop in the Wiltshire village where I live that the Polish Golden Arrow has been entrusted, and you will have to read this story in order to find out what this means!

If, after you have read this book, you are able to say, "Now I know things about the Chief and about Scouting and Guiding which I never knew before", this story will not have been written in vain.

M. de B.

PART I
THE BOY
"STE"

ONCE UPON A TIME there was a boy. He had several brothers, and we meet them for the first time on board their ten-ton sailing boat. It is a lovely calm day, with the sun shining brightly and seagulls wheeling and crying overhead. The boat is at anchor just off-shore and the boys have landed from a dinghy and are exploring the beach. One of them, sandy-haired and freckled, has stopped exploring and is lying on his back, thinking. His knees are drawn up, and the soft, warm, wet sand is squelching through his toes. He has been reading about pirates in an old book given to his brother by their father, and there is one particular pirate captain who is a great hero of his. This pirate's name is "One-Eyed Bill", of the *Lovely Mary*; and he has taught the boy a lot of things. He could splice, and sing, and take care of himself in a ship at sea, and had been round the world many times. He had lost his right arm, so he had learnt to do things equally well with his left. He could cook his own food, and understand the ways of birds and animals. In fact, he was a very all-round sort of fellow, and the boy who lay on the sand was thinking that one day, when he was a man, he would like to be as good a man as Pirate Bill.

He lay there thinking of what he could do, and he came to the conclusion that, up to date, he had acquired quite a number of Pirate Bill's accomplishments. As a small child he was always devoted to animals and birds, and he learnt to imitate their cries. He used to cut out pictures of animals to amuse his brothers and sister, and he would draw pictures of maps with his right hand, and paint them with his left. Once when he and his brothers were in the country for a holiday, they made houses in the trees, and learnt to build huts with furze and bracken. They could cook their own food, skin a rabbit, and make different kinds of camp fires.

As the boy lay thinking of all this he realised that what he wanted most was to explore the world, to go about and see everything. All adventures in boats were very thrilling and wonderful things. He and his brothers had already been into many harbours on the South Coast in the sailing boat that was now rocking lazily on the coming tide.

Then someone shouted "Come on, Ste!" You may perhaps be wondering about the boy's name. It was Robert Stevenson Smythe Baden-Powell—always known by his family as "Ste". His day-dreams about pirates and adventures were over for the moment, but his last thought was that he would like to be a soldier best, because soldiers saw foreign seas and foreign lands as well, and theirs was a great life.

The brothers had soon embarked, and away they went cruising along the coast. Suddenly, as so often happens on a quiet and peaceful sunny day, the sky grew overcast. A sudden squall came down upon them. The sea got very rough. The wind turned to a gale. The boys had their work cut out to keep the boat on a level keel. They were rather frightened and felt seasick, but the eldest gave orders which they obeyed without question. So they reached port safely. The adventure over, they felt that it had been thoroughly worth while.

Ste went to school at Charterhouse. His schooldays were full of life. He was a keen and good actor, but he was never conceited about what he did, and looked upon most of it as tremendous fun. He had many friends, and was always popular because he was not afraid to get into a scrape and own up afterwards. This was one reason why he made friends with the schoolmasters as well as the boys. It was not unnatural that when he grew up his old schoolmasters still continued to be his friends.

"Nowadays you often hear boys and girls running down their teachers. They have rude and stupid nicknames for them and do everything they can to give them a bad time. This is a great pity, because no great adventure is complete unless we can make friends with people who can teach us things, and people who have spent their lives learning in order that they may pass on knowledge to other people deserve a good deal of respect and gratitude from the young beggars they are trying to teach." These words were written by Ste many years later.

Here is one story of his schooldays. On one occasion. at a school entertainment, a promised performer failed to put in an appearance. The boys were getting rather impatient, so the headmaster turned to B.-P., who was sitting near to him, and asked if he could do something to fill up the gap. Without turning a hair the boy rose, got on to the stage and began to recount some episodes of school life, keeping the other boys in roars of laughter with his take-off of a French lesson. Fortunately, the French master was not present.

Years afterwards the headmaster, when speaking of Baden-Powell, said that he was always full of pranks, but that the chief reason for his popularity with boys and masters alike was that whatever he did he always owned up at once and took whatever punishment was coming to him with a grin. Schooldays were good days. He worked hard and played hard. Every free moment he had in the holidays he spent with dogs or horses, or just out in the woods and fields, climbing and exploring, cooking his own food, or just lying on his back with his face to the sky, thinking.

PART II

THE SOLDIER

INDIA

When he was nineteen Baden-Powell left school. He had not definitely meant to be a soldier, but sat for the army examination, and as he passed this with flying colours he received a direct commission in the 13th Hussars and was sent straight out to India.

He found his brother officers a very fine set of men, and the 13th Hussars being a famous cavalry regiment, he was able to gratify his great love for horses. He rode a great deal, usually "Patience", his favourite chestnut mare. She would come to him when he called her, and he had taught her to stand quietly without being tied up. A horse-dealer came along one day and asked if he would sell her. His answer was, "You try and ride her." The mare was standing quietly, looking very gentle and peaceful. The man—who fancied himself as a horseman—started to mount. Down went the mare's head, her back formed a beautiful arch, and with one buck she had him on the ground. She repeated this trick three times, as her master had taught her to do. The dealer went away thoroughly disgusted, much to the amusement of the young subaltern Baden-Powell.

He had a way with animals and children, and even

wild things seemed to know instinctively that he would not hurt them. At this time in India he had a fox terrier called "Beetle". He was a grand little dog and very game. Beetle would sit at the edge of the polo field during matches. He never ran on to the ground, and was always the first to welcome his master after a match. In the final of a cup competition Baden-Powell was to ride Patience as one of his mounts. He got on to the field and, looking round, realised that Beetle was not there. He ran back to the stables, to find Beetle, barking furiously, shut up in one of the boxes. As he let him out he said: "The three of us must be together the day our team wins the cup." And they won it, with Patience carrying him to victory and Beetle to watch from the side of the ground.

His soldiering days in India were varied and full, and he was tremendously interested in all he saw. There were months spent in the hill country, up on the North-West Frontier. On one occasion he was sent on an expedition with native troops. The days were extremely hot and the nights bitterly cold. Early dawn saw the troops in camp high up on a rocky shelf, with the great plain spread below them. The commanding officer sent for Baden-Powell and ordered him to take an Indian soldier to reconnoitre the enemy outposts and bring back information. This was a mission worth undertaking and a dangerous one at that.

He was to be ready to start in half an hour. He had made a practice ever since he came to India of having his kit absolutely ready for any emergency, so that at short notice he would always be ready to start off without delay. He had taught the men under his command to do the same thing. On this occasion the commanding officer was surprised to see Baden-Powell waiting and completely prepared to start ten minutes after he had received his orders. In conversation afterwards with a famous general he said, in referring to this incident: "That young man will go very far in the army, as he has learnt to be prepared for any emergency."

B.-P. started off at dawn. There were hillsides to climb in the blazing midday heat, and rough stony paths to follow along the edge of precipices, and at last Baden-Powell and his companion reached the neighbourhood of the enemy camp. They had to cover the last part of the journey by careful stalking, and B.-P. decided that he would leave the Indian behind, disguise himself as a blind beggar and go into the enemy camp alone. He spoke the language well, and he managed to make himself look about as dirty and disreputable as any beggar. He put a few small pebbles in his mouth so that his voice was indistinct. He had practised this on previous occasions. He then advanced boldly. He remained with the enemy for twenty-four hours. They decided that he was old and probably half-witted, and took very little notice of him, except to throw him a few scraps of food and some coins.

Having discovered all that he wished to know, he returned only to find that the Indian, probably thinking that he was dead, had left. Now, this man knew the way and had guided Baden-Powell. As he had run away it meant that there was nothing for it but for the young officer to find his own way back to the British camp. Then it was that he put into practice all those things that he had learnt as a boy. One particular practice that stood him in good stead all his life was a habit of looking back occasionally to see what the country looked like from the opposite angle. He had taken certain landmarks as he went along and made a mental note of them. It took him three days to get back to the British camp. After this escapade, when recommended for promotion, he wrote to his mother: "But it was not the promotion, it was the fun of the thing, seeing the enemy being hoodwinked, and I nearly laughed once or twice when they chucked me their scraps of food. This is the sort of thing I call an adventure."

His letters home at this time were full of yarns showing how much he enjoyed the comradeship of these camping expeditions. He often spoke of the camp fires at night under the stars, and of the friendships formed between men of all sorts and kinds. The camping side of a soldier's life meant a tremendous lot to him. He was always the handyman, and knew how to be comfortable and to show other people how to be so, too. He reminded his mother of the camping holidays with his brothers when they were all boys together. "They were grand days," he would say. "But this"—meaning India and soldiering—"is the real thing."

Again we see B.-P. on the North-West Frontier. Posted to a new station, he noticed that the men of a famous regiment quartered there were of different castes and races, but that they had certain things in common. They were all, without exception, big, strong and physically fit, and like all good men, they said very little and got on with the job. Their duties consisted mainly of going on very dangerous expeditions. When any duty was exceptionally dangerous, and the men were literally taking their lives in their hands, volunteers were asked for. Such an occasion happened shortly after B.-P. had been stationed there, and he was particularly struck by the fact that far more men than were needed had volunteered, and that those who could not be accepted were bitterly disappointed.

Another outstanding point about these men was that when they were off duty they were always training themselves physically and mentally. One of their British officers remarked with reference to this constant training: "You must be prepared in a place like this because you never know what may happen." This remark remained in B.-P.'s memory for many years, and comes into our story later.

This regiment was always stationed on the North-West Frontier, and was called the GUIDES—because its duty was to go ahead and reconnoitre for others to follow. No one who sets out on a duty of that kind dare be anything but physically fit. B.-P. was particularly struck with the cheerfulness of these men, and their courage. Years afterwards he used to say that it was a lesson in itself just to live with them. They could cook a meal under any circumstances. They were good at all kinds of signalling. They did not neglect those most important things—a knowledge of first aid and nursing. Above all, they had a simple faith in God.

OBSERVATION TESTS

THESE Indian days were good days for B.-P., but at last the time came when his regiment was ordered home. Some trouble was feared in South Africa, so their transports were stopped at Port Natal and they disembarked there. When B.-P. set foot on the African continent he little thought how well he was to know that country and how much he would grow to love it.

The Colonel gave him a special job. He had to pretend to be an ordinary traveller and ride six hundred miles up-country collecting information. During this trip he got to know the Boers very well, and he learned to admire them for many reasons, chiefly because they were very independent, and if they undertook a job they would carry it through, no matter how many difficulties they had to face. There were two other things that B.-P.

admired about them: firstly, they were magnificent horsemen; and secondly, they could use a rifle, and use it well.

B.-P. adopted an interesting method of making notes. Instead of writing everything down, he used to draw pictures. This was copied from a Red Indian idea and was a kind of sign language. For instance, he might do a drawing of a river, a group of trees, some mountains, a rifle, a camp fire, some deer and a lake. This would mean that he had crossed a river, passed by a group of trees, gone over the mountains and made camp where there was food to be had, and water. He always drew pictorial maps of the country he passed through, and made special reference to, and accurate descriptions of, anyone he met and spoke to, whether they were natives or white men. He always carried handfuls of beads, one or two cheap watches, and some coloured ribbon, and with these he made friends with the tribesmen, whom he treated no differently from white men, at all times showing the same courtesy and consideration. In consequence, he got the best out of them.

In the end the trouble that had been anticipated did not break out. B.-P. was ordered back to England with his regiment. He was delighted to be home. He used to say, in later life, that that first home-coming, after India and Africa, made him realise what home really meant, and how dear it was to him. When we see the English spring come, year after year, we who live here don't always appreciate it, but we can imagine B.-P., with his love of the country, appreciating it to the full. He worked hard with his regiment, but when he got leave he would go touring about England enjoying the scenery and studying the countryside. The love of adventure continually called to him, so he welcomed the opportunity, when it came, to do intelligence work in Russia and Germany. He used to tell the story of meeting an old diplomat who, in conversation with him one day, remarked: "You are young, but you have a very quiet voice. You say little and see much. You will go far, because you will command men. No one commands by shouting. Great men command by little speech and much thought." At the time B.-P. did not believe this to be true, because he was very modest, but he said, when telling me this story years afterwards, that although he did not feel that he had achieved this high standard, it made him do his best to attain it.

DINIZULU'S NECKLACE

By now B.-P. was getting well forward in his career, and he was seconded to go to Capetown as A.D.C. with his uncle. Soon afterwards trouble broke out with the Zulus under their Chief, Dinizulu.

This chief was a very clever man, and he had a necklace made of about a thousand wooden beads, which he wore round his neck on state occasions. Dinizulu was six foot seven, so you may imagine the length of the necklace which, when wound twice round his neck, still touched the ground. It was a sacred symbol of the tribe, and was kept in a particular cave and guarded night and day. There was a saying amongst Dinizulu's warriors that all resistance would end if the necklace was ever stolen. B.-P. got to hear of this, and all through the campaign he hoped he would have the luck to capture the Great Chief himself and get his necklace. There were many dangers during this fighting with the Zulu warriors, for they were not only clever in knowing every inch of their wild country, but they could hide themselves like wild animals, and would lie in wait and ambush the men looking for them. So our soldiers, and B.-P. in particular as their leader, had to be tremendously alert, quick of eye and foot, and also immensely brave, penetrating into that unknown bit of country.

Eventually the Zulus gave themselves up, and B.-P. got the coveted necklace, which will come into this story again.

He had learned a great deal about tracking from actual experience during this long trek, and had studied the African men's habits and ways quite a lot. He was specially interested in the boys of the Zulu and Swazi tribes in South Africa, who had to learn to be scouts before they could be allowed to be considered men. These boys, when about fifteen or sixteen, were taken by the men of the village, stripped of their clothes and painted white from head to foot. Then they were given a shield and one small spear, turned out of the village, and told that they would be killed if anyone caught them while they were still painted white. So these boys had to go off into the jungle and mountains and hide themselves for about a month until the white paint wore off. All this time they had to learn stalking, observation, fire-lighting by rubbing sticks together, making clothes with the skins of the animals they had killed, and finding out what roots, berries and trees were good for food. The boy who could not do this died or was killed. The boy who came back to his village when the white paint had worn off was received with great rejoicing, and allowed to become a man of the tribe. It seems a cruel test, but the tribesmen realised how necessary it was that a boy should not think that he was necessarily a man because he was grown up. In speaking of this in after-years B.-P. said: "Boys should be trained in manliness. They must know what it is not to whine at hardship, and they must not be allowed to drift into being poor-spirited wasters who can only look on while men work."

You can imagine the thought of these African boys

going through B.-P.'s mind as he rode about the wide and beautiful African Veldt. He was quite young himself, full of courage and well trained in the arts of scouting and observation. He had learnt these things years ago with his brothers in the good hard days when he was a youngster.

It was during the Zulu Campaign that B.-P. heard the Zulu Impi, or Zulu soldiers, sing the Een-Gonyama Chorus. He was very taken with this. It was always sung in honour of some great hunter or chief. Here are the words:

> "Een-Gonyama, Gonyama Invooboo
> Yabo Yabo Invooboo."

This means:

> "He is a lion, he is a lion.
> No, he is greater than a lion: he is
> hippopotamus."

There is a splendid tune to this song, and years afterwards B.-P. used to teach boys to sing it.

Then came a period in B.-P.'s career when for a time he was stationed at Malta, and from there he had a chance of doing more intelligence work in the Balkans and Turkey. After this he returned to his old regiment, the 13th Hussars. He was stationed in Ireland, in the 'County of the Short Grass'—better known as County Kildare. He had some grand horses at the time and did a great deal of riding. One old General, who admired B.-P.'s powers of horsemanship, once said of him: "He wins many races, but he'd rather lose than kill his horse in a steeplechase."

Many young fellows who are keen about horses might take to heart the old General's remarks. Whatever fun B.-P. got out of his animals, he was never hard on them, and always cared for them better than the sport they could give him.

While stationed in Ireland, B.-P. showed how resourceful he was in big manœuvres of troops. When commanding a side he was always very original, and invariably did the unexpected thing. This took the 'enemy' by surprise. The Commander-in-Chief was so impressed with B.-P.'s knowledge and the way he put it into practice, that when an expedition had to be sent to Ashanti B.-P. was specially chosen to go out with it. When appointed he followed his usual practice. First of all he looked over his kit, seeing that everything was in perfect order, and not leaving someone else to do it all for him. Secondly, he made sure that he was perfectly fit. One of the chief reasons why he always got such a good result from medical exams. was because he never did anything to excess—eating, drinking, etc.

He had never smoked, because he felt it would impair his sense of smell, and in Africa many a time his acute sense of smell had been a great help in locating camps and animals. He was, however, advised to smoke on this trip to keep away the mosquitoes!

When he got to Ashanti he was put in charge of some rather unruly and quite uneducated men. They had not been handled well, and were lazy, and needed a lot of training to be of use on the expedition. B.-P. discovered quite by chance that the one thing these people loved was that a white man should give them a strange name. He therefore started giving them names all round—"Tar Bucket", "Glue", "Soap", "Bounder", "Brass Pan", "Pea Soup", "Whatnot", "Poor Beggar", etc. Every man who was enrolled was given a name, and if they did anything wrong B.-P. refused to call them by that name as a punishment. This was a very clever idea, and the men learned to love and respect him because he was just and fair, and he found that by cheering them on with a little praise when they did well he could get a lot more out of them.

As a result the Africans would do anything for B.-P., and he got very strenuous work done quickly. This consisted mainly of making roads. If anything, B.-P. worked harder than his men. At one time the road the men were making led through some terribly difficult country. The men got very downhearted, and there was some grumbling. B.-P. got them all together and had what was called a 'palaver'. He stood up and addressed them: "We are as the eyes and body of a great snake which is crawling up the bush path from the coast and is coiling for its spring. The eyes of the snake are hungry. The snake is brave and he does not allow his stomach to conquer him, so he will go on until he reaches Kumassi, and on that day there will be a great feast and much meat." The Africans all laughed at this strange illustration. They liked the idea of being a great snake. The snake was an animal that was much admired in that particular part of the country. One of their chiefs stepped forward and said that they wished to do great honour to the white soldier, so they would christen him 'The Head of the Snake'.

The great road which B.-P. and his local recruits built extended nearly two hundred miles through swampy country covered with bush and forest. To build it they had to clear trees, build bridges, and construct huts. B.-P. showed that he had a first-class knowledge of pioneering by the time the road was made. It was during this expedition that, for the first time, he wore the famed Stetson, or Cowboy, hat. The Africans gave him yet another nickname: 'Kantankye', which means 'He of the Big Hat'. It was here, too, that B.-P. got into the habit of carrying a staff marked with feet and inches. He found it very useful for crossing streams, making measurements, and walking through swamps.

There was very little actual fighting during the Ashanti

expedition. King Prempeh was taken by surprise when the expedition arrived, and was taken prisoner quite easily. All his practices of putting people to torture and to death were stopped, and the country afterwards became quiet and prosperous.

B.-P. had got into the habit of using an expression which was really a West African saying. He said afterwards that it often stood him in good stead. Perhaps some of us might find it useful nowadays: 'Softly, softly, catchee monkey.' In other words, if you are trying to lead anyone, convince anyone, or get anyone on your side, go at it gently, and tactfully, and you stand a very good chance to 'catchee monkey'.

IMPEESA

B.-P. HAD rendered great service to his country, and he was promoted to Brevet Lieutenant-Colonel. However, he had only been home and stationed in Ireland a short time when he was given yet another job. In writing home to his mother about this appointment, many years later, he called it 'the best adventure of my life'. At that time the country which we now call Rhodesia was called Matabeleland. The Matabele—a very strong tribe and really fine people—had started a rebellion, and B.-P. was appointed chief of staff to the officer commanding the British Forces which were sent to quell the rising.

One of the chief difficulties of fighting the Matabele was that they did not come out into the open for battle. They fought in small parties, hiding in the very rough wild country and harassing the British with constant small attacks. The only way to meet this type of tribal warfare, which largely consisted of good and skilled scouting, was to adopt the same methods. B.-P. since the earliest days of his army career had shown that he was an exceptionally good scout. During the Matabele Campaign he put all the best of his scouting into operation and was so good at the game that the Africans became afraid of him and looked upon him with superstitious dread. They bestowed a great honour upon him, for it was during this campaign that he received the nickname 'Impeesa', meaning 'The Wolf that Never Sleeps'. He was also called 'M'lala-Pahnsi', meaning 'The Man who Sits Tight', or 'The Man who Lies Down to Shoot', or 'The Man who does not Hurry'. All of which goes to prove that B.-P. was much respected, even by his enemies. He often said that he bore a charmed life during the Matabele Campaign and that one of the reasons why he was never shot, though some of the Africans had firearms, was because the Matabele were determined to catch him alive in order to put into practice the hideous tortures that they had devised for him.

On one occasion an old tribesman he met offered to show him the way to an enemy hiding place in the rocky hillsides. B.-P. had been out for many hours and was dog-tired. He hesitated, wondering if he could trust the old man. There was a piece of information which he particularly wanted, and if he followed that man he would be bound to get it. So he decided to take the risk. However, with his usual caution, he kept his eyes open, being careful not to let the old man see that he was being closely watched. He noticed after a time that the man kept putting his hand into a skin bag that he was carrying. B.-P. pretended to be lame, and dropped behind for a moment. He then saw the African was dropping red seed pods at intervals as he went along. Without saying a word and quite noiselessly B.-P. slipped off the trail, climbed through some rough scrub and lay down on the top of a slight rise in some bushes. He saw the man start and look round for him and finally sit down as if waiting. B.-P. remained hidden, and, sure enough, after about half an hour, a party of Matabele, fully armed, came noiselessly along, following the trail of seed pods. They seemed very angry when they met the old man waving his arms and talking excitedly, but B.-P. was too far away to hear what they had to say. He did not dare to move, in case they should hear or smell him, as these Africans had ears and noses as sensitive as animals. He lay watching the trail and at last the Matabele dispersed and began to hunt for him, and there followed a tremendous chase. Had he not been physically fit he would undoubtedly have been caught. The short rest had revived him, and luckily it was getting dark, so he managed to escape them. No wonder they called him 'The Wolf that Never Sleeps'. A brother officer asked him later what made him suspect the old man who was guiding him. B.-P. answered: "I didn't exactly suspect him. I had an uncomfortable feeling because he never looked at me when he spoke to me. And secondly, 'Be Prepared' is a good motto." B.-P. little knew then how famous that motto was to become, although he so often used it long before Scouting for Boys was thought of.

NOTHING BUT THE BEST

B.-P. WAS appointed Colonel in command of the 5th Dragoon Guards after the Matabele Campaign was over. The regiment was in India, so he found himself there once more. He was perhaps one of the most popular commanding officers of his time. There were many reasons for this, but the most important was that he never asked anyone to do anything that he was not prepared to do himself, and that he treated officers and men alike as friends and as individuals. It was one man to another. Everyone got a square deal from B.-P. This does not mean that he was not a hard taskmaster. 'Nothing but the best' was his favourite saying at that time. His regiment must be second to none. If a man did anything wrong, if he was lazy or dishonest, or dirty and slovenly in his personal appearance, B.-P. was down on him like a ton of bricks. The men knew that he was equally hard on himself, and that even his riding—which was always his favourite recreation and consisted of breaking young horses, polo ponies, pig-sticking and hunting—was only done in his own spare time, and never at the expense of the regiment.

He took a great deal of trouble about the entertainment of the troops, and he used to act in concerts and plays. One day at a concert a Private Brown was announced, a visitor from another regiment, who got up to perform, and did it very badly indeed. The performance was so poor that the soldiers in the audience greeted it with shouts and catcalls of derision. Poor Private Brown, looking very unhappy and depressed, said, as a parting shot, that he thought it was most unkind to treat a fellow in this way. Then someone near the front said: "That was B.-P.!", whereat the commanding officer disclosed his real identity amid roars of laughter.

At this time B.-P. began to put a great deal more scouting into the regiment's training. He divided the men into small teams or patrols under an N.C.O. When they had learned their scouting they went in for competitions against each other. B.-P. got permission for the men to be awarded a proficiency badge for good scouting. This proficiency badge was an arrowhead, rather like that at the end of the north part of a compass. Someone once described it as meaning 'Keep right on to the end of the road'.

About this time, in India, B.-P. wrote a book called

Aids to Scouting, but it was not published until later, when it was to prove immensely useful in the army and in what was afterwards the Boy Scout Movement. He enjoyed this time in his army life as much as any, and when he went on leave he wrote with characteristic humility to his brother officers saying: "I'm so grateful to you chaps, because you've taught me so much."

And so we find him in England for a brief spell of holiday, meeting his old friends and reunited with his family; but it was not till later in his life that he was really to enjoy England.

CO-OPERATION

The call came suddenly, and within a few weeks of arriving home the Commander-in-Chief of the Home Forces sent for B.-P. and asked if he could go to South Africa on the following Saturday. The answer came at once: "No, Sir, I'm afraid I can't." This caused some surprise, but B.-P. hastily added: "There's no boat on Saturday, but there is on Friday. Shall I go then?"

Thus it was decided in a few simple words that B.-P. should set out on one of the greatest adventures of his life. There was a possibility that war would soon break out in South Africa between the Boers and the British. In the event of such a war it was important that certain frontiers should be guarded. Rhodesia (Matabeleland) and Bechuanaland had to be defended at all costs. This would be one of the most important parts of the campaign, and B.-P. was sent for.

The fact of the matter was that, although the South African war was not declared, B.-P. had been told that it was imminent. He had also been told that it was imperative that two mounted regiments should be raised and trained in a few months, and so, without any fuss, he set out to do the job. He picked his men very carefully. They had not only to be skilled horsemen, but they had to have a knowledge of veterinary work, the care of horses and even be trained as farriers. B.-P. himself could shoe a horse. It was important that the men should understand the training of raw remounts. If B.-P. ever found a man rough-handling a horse or losing his temper when breaking it, that man had to go. The horses of these two regiments and the men who looked after them were the finest force that has ever been raised for the type of job to be undertaken.

Years after, when B.-P. was talking over the campaign with a brother officer who had been with him at the time, he told this story:

"There was one fellow in particular whom I always liked to have with me if we were in a tight corner. He was very nearly as fond of a horse as I am. One night he came to me after a skirmish, looking terribly serious. 'I've got very bad news for you, Sir,' he said. I was expecting a message from the General, so I thought that the bad news concerned the campaign, but I was wrong. In a few halting words the man explained that 'Nobby' was dead. I afterwards found out that this man had sat up with him for five days and nights without sleep. The horse was suffering from some kind of local horse sickness."

Continuing his talk with the same brother officer, B.-P. summed it all up by saying: "One of the chief reasons for the success of these two irregular cavalry regiments was that the men loved the horses and the horses came first with them. They were treated like children, and they responded by showing as much devotion to duty as the men themselves. I'd like to see every boy in this country have a horse of his own, train it himself, and learn to look after it as those fellows did in South Africa. Some of my soldiers were mere boys, and half the time it was the horses that made men of them."

The training that these men went through was strenuous in the extreme. There was very little time, and B.-P. adopted his own method of working in small teams or patrols with a leader who was responsible to the commanding officer for his patrol. The manœuvres undertaken were severe and difficult, and no man spared himself. His methods, however, proved most successful. He commanded one regiment himself, and the other was under Colonel Plumer, who had been with B.-P. during the Matabele Campaign. Colonel Plumer himself was a very fine horseman, and keen about B.-P.'s methods of training. He afterwards became one of his greatest friends.

When at last war with South Africa was certain, the Commander-in-Chief approached Colonel Baden-Powell and was informed, and indeed saw for himself, that two perfectly trained regiments, ready for the field, were available for the defence of Rhodesia and Bechuanaland. This was a triumph of organisation and leadership. At the time B.-P., in his usual clever way, did an amusing drawing of a row of army horses standing together and talking of the events of the day. A little farther away was a group of cavalrymen. The cavalrymen were made to say: "We should never 'ave done it without the 'osses." The horses were made to say: "It was a bit of luck that we happened to get the best cavalrymen in the British Army to pull us through." The Chief called the picture 'Co-operation'.

THE LEATHER BOOTLACE

TURMOIL and excitement! War was declared. Plumer was sent with one regiment to Rhodesia; B.-P. made his

The First Lord Baden-Powell of Gilwell
Portrait by Shirley Slocombe 1916

B-P playing his kudu horn, first used at
Brownsea Island Camp in 1907

The Chief Scout with scouts from 23 countries at Wembley Paddocks Camp, August 1924

The Chiefs

headquarters in the little town of Mafeking. At once a Boer General with a large army advanced on Mafeking. They thought that a small garrison could not possibly hold out for long, and they came over the veldt with what B.-P. described in his diary as "a sort of swagger that puts a man's back up". Mafeking had no natural defences of any kind, and a tremendous lot of work had to be done constructing and improvising fortifications, digging trenches and putting up earthworks.

It was a great ordeal for the people who lived in Mafeking, and there were about fifteen hundred white people and about eight thousand Africans. The actual garrison consisted of about twelve hundred men, who were badly armed and had artillery that was out of date. B.-P. wrote in his diary at the time: "Found small boys playing soldiers with the only available six guns; about all they were any good for!" Two other guns were used in Mafeking later on. One was made in the railway workshop and was nicknamed 'The Wolf'. The other one was very old and, strangely enough, was found in the town being used as a gatepost. It was removed from this position and mounted on framework. While this was being done the initials of the makers, Bailey and Pegg, were discovered on it. The initials were BP, and everyone felt that this was a good omen and must bring the garrison luck.

The Boers, on the other hand, had excellent guns of the latest type, some of them quite large siege guns. It has always been a mystery how B.-P. managed to hold Mafeking, but there are undoubtedly two particular things that made this possible—two special characteristics of B.-P.'s own nature. The first one was summed up in the words that he used to say to his men when training them: "If you don't know, invent. In other words, use your brain to outwit the other fellow." The second was B.-P.'s sense of humour, which never deserted him even in the gloomiest moments of the siege.

The Boers knew that the Matabele was a great fighting race, full of skill and resource. They knew also of the reputation that B.-P. had amongst the Matabele, who had called him 'The Wolf that Never Sleeps'. During the siege of Mafeking the tiny British garrison was facing overwhelming odds, but they had a leader on whom they could rely; a man who did not stand and give orders, but who gave orders and proceeded at once to carry them out himself. The Africans had confidence in him, and said that the gods of the white men had smiled when he was born.

Whatever was going on, you may be sure that B.-P. was the life and soul of it. Even during the siege, to relieve the tension for the people he encouraged them to get up concerts and entertainments; and although his anxiety at times was almost unbearable, he never shared it with anybody. Any kind of night attack was the most dangerous thing of all. B.-P. invented all sorts of stunts to hoodwink the Boers. There was very little dynamite in the town, but B.-P. ordered a mine to be laid. This looked like a heap of sand. A great many other mines were also laid, but only the first one had dynamite in it. All the others were dummy heaps of sand, but they let the enemy know about them to prevent their approach. Actually the one mine exploded when a man passed it on a bicycle and he was killed—he had disobeyed instructions and had gone close to it even though warned not to. The Boers, however, saw the accident happen and were very careful after this, and did not dare to come too near the town at night. They little knew that there was no more dynamite available, and it was very lucky for the people in the besieged town that the ruse succeeded.

Another clever idea was to make a searchlight out of a sheet of tin and an old acetylene lamp. This was lit and placed on a pole at a certain spot. After a while it was extinguished and rushed hurriedly to another place, where it was again turned on. This went on all night, and the Boers got the impression that the defenders had a whole battery of searchlights. This also prevented them from approaching too near at night.

Warfare was a very different thing in those days, as you will see from the fact that by mutual agreement Sundays were off-days for both sides. The Boers used to come out of their defences and climb over their barbed-wire entanglements. The British garrison had not enough barbed wire to go round, so B.-P. made them do some acting and pretend that they were climbing over barbed wire. This needed some practice, but they managed to take the Boers in. One Boer who was taken prisoner admitted that his comrades thought that the British had tremendous barbed-wire entanglements.

For weeks on end B.-P. would hardly allow himself any rest or sleep at night. He was always thinking out new ways of outwitting the other fellow and of keeping everyone cheerful. He used to go out alone at night on scouting expeditions, and at last, when the Boers made an attack and were severely punished and driven off with considerable loss, they learned to respect 'The Wolf that Never Sleeps'. Food was so scarce that all the horses had to be eaten.

There were a number of boys living in the town and a specially selected few were collected together and turned into a corps of messengers. They were divided up into patrols and given leaders. B.-P. and his officers believed in these boys and used them to carry messages and letters from one part of the town to the other and to do quite valuable work. There was one particular boy who did very daring things on a bicycle. One day when he had ridden through a hail of bullets B.-P. ticked him off and told him not to be so reckless. The boy replied: "Sorry, Sir, but I go so fast that they would never catch me." One of the special arrangements that was made for carrying on the services of the town was the designing of a pound note and the printing of stamps. One of these stamps had the drawing of a boy on a bicycle. B.-P. used to say afterwards: "They were splendid chaps, ragamuffins perhaps, but give me a ragamuffin when you are in a tight corner." That drawing that B.-P. did of a ragamuffin on a bicycle, which was afterwards put on a stamp, turned the ragamuffins into heroes, which they really were.

It was not often that B.-P. allowed himself to get depressed, but there must have been times when his spirits were low, because as time went on conditions became very bad in the town. However, one of his favourite sayings always was: 'It is darkest just before the dawn'. He had an invariable practice of going round the defences each morning to speak to the men on their posts. Often he had himself been out scouting in the enemy's lines during the night, but he was out and about as usual the next morning. One morning while on his rounds he saw an old African 'boy' who was employed as a scavenger, and greeted him. This meeting of the highest and the lowest in the garrison was no unusual occurrence. In Mafeking all were defenders, and on a level as such. The 'boy' stopped and said: "Baas, every morning when I see you I have heard you whistling and seen you smiling. Today you are not smiling, not whistling. Why is that? What has happened?" The reply came: "Every day I am full of hope, but today, for some reason that I do not know, I cannot see ahead into the future." The 'boy' took from round his neck a leather thong and placed it in B.-P.'s hands, saying: "Baas, when I was born my mother tied this thong round my neck to keep off evil spirits and to bring me good fortune. I am old and I will not require it any more. You are young. Take it so that fortune may come to you, and I may see you smile and hear you whistle again each morning." B.-P. took the thong and placed it in the pocket of his tunic with a word of thanks and a smile. That day news came by heliograph that Colonel Plumer's relieving column hoped to get through to them within a week. The thong given to B.-P. by the old African tribesman that early morning on the ramparts of Mafeking was to make history. It will come into this story again along with some other things that have been mentioned, and which stand rather like signposts along the trail of B.-P.'s life. So look out later for the Leather Bootlace.

At last Mafeking was relieved. Plumer's men were approaching from the north, but another force under Colonel Mahon came up from the south and entered the town just before they were completely out of food. One of the first men to enter the town was B.-P.'s youngest brother. It was known how serious the situation had become, and he had specially volunteered to go with the relieving force. In telling the story of the relief of Mafeking, B.-P., who was always very modest about his achievements, merely said: "When it was all over I just had time to thank God before I fell asleep; and it was a long sleep."

After the relief of Mafeking B.-P. was made a Major-General. He had rendered conspicuous service to his country, and the Queen showed him much appreciation. He had carried through a tough job, and after taking further part in the campaign for some months, he was called once more to tackle a great undertaking. He was to raise and train a body of men to do the policing of the country after the war was over. This body was called the South African Constabulary.

THE SOUTH AFRICAN CONSTABULARY

ORGANISING a body of men like the South African Constabulary was a tremendous bit of work. The idea was to train a band of men to be what B.-P. called 'Peace Scouts'. Here are his own words, written many years after the South African Constabulary was started, and when B.-P. was trying to teach boys and girls how to be happy and make the best of their lives:

> "A Scout, as you know, is generally a soldier who is chosen for his cleverness and pluck to go out in front of an army in war to find out where the enemy are and report to the commander all about them. But besides war scouts there are also peace scouts. Men who in peace-time carry out work which requires the same kind of ability. These are the frontiersmen of all parts of our Empire: the trappers of North America, hunters of Central Africa, pioneers, missionaries, explorers all over Asia, and all the wild parts of the world. The bushmen and drovers of Australia, the mounted police of North-West Canada, and the South African Constabulary. All are peace scouts, real men in every sense of the word and thoroughly up in scoutcraft. They understand living out in jungles, and they can find their way anywhere. They are able to read meanings from the smallest signs and foot-tracks; they know how to look after their health when far away from any doctors, are strong and plucky, and ready to face any danger, and always keen to help each other. They are accustomed to take their lives in their hands and to fling them down

without any hesitation if they can help their country by doing so. They give up everything, their personal comforts and desires, in order to get their work done. They do not do this for their own amusement, but because it is their duty. . . . The history of the British Empire has been made by adventurers and explorers, the scouts of the nation, for hundreds of years past. The Knights of King Arthur, Richard Cœur-de-Lion, and the Crusaders carried British chivalry into distant parts of the earth. Raleigh, Drake, and Captain John Smith, soldiers and sailors of Queen Elizabeth's time, faced unknown dangers of strange seas, as well as the known danger of powerful enemies, to take and hold new lands for the expansion of our small kingdom. Captain Cook in Australia, Lord Clive in India, opened up new countries. Speke, Baker, and Livingstone pushed their way through the savage deserts and forests of Africa; Davis, Franklin, and Ross braved the ice and snows of the Arctic regions; and more lately, Scott and Shackleton gave their lives in scouting in the Antarctic.

"These are just a few out of the hundreds of the scouts of our own nation who have from all times down to the present spread the good name and power of our country to all parts of the world.

"There have been women scouts of the nation, too, such as Grace Darling, who risked her life to save a shipwrecked crew; Florence Nightingale, who nursed sick soldiers in the Crimean War; Miss Kingsley, the African explorer; Lady Lugard in Africa and Alaska; and many devoted lady missionaries and nurses in all parts of our Empire. These have shown that women and girls as well as men and boys may well learn scouting when they are young and so be able to do useful work in the world as they grow older.

> "It is a grand life, but it cannot suddenly be taken up by any man or woman who thinks that he or she would like it. They must prepare themselves for it beforehand." (*Scouting for Boys.*)

Let us take the outstanding points from the yarn which has just been quoted. The peace scouts were trained in stalking, and tracking, and observation. They had to be fit and healthy, which made them strong and able to do their job. They had to learn to make decisions for themselves, to keep calm in the face of danger, to give up pleasure and comfort in the cause of their duty, and above all they had to be ready and keen to help each other. Take special note of these things. They were the foundations upon which B.-P. trained the South African Constabulary. They turned out a magnificent set of men, many of whom, owing to the training he gave them, were able to become leaders themselves.

On his return to England B.-P. was given other appointments, amongst them that of Inspector-General of Cavalry. His experience in training and organising the South African Constabulary stood him in good stead, and his knowledge and love of horses made him an inspector-general whose opinion was very much respected by all under him. He made a habit of remaining with different cavalry regiments for some days at a stretch, and he insisted upon seeing the men exercising and looking after their horses in the stable as well as, what he called, 'spat on and polished-up on the parade ground'. His vast experience of training men always led him to the same conclusion. They must be healthy, keen, brave and decent to the other men with whom they had to work. His army career was drawing to a close, and in it he had fulfilled all his desires as a boy.

PART III

THE SCOUT

SCOUTING FOR BOYS

ALL through his many years of army life B.-P. had made a habit of keeping a diary. It came easily to him to write things that he had done and heard and seen, and he had that very rare gift, the ability when he once started a thing to keep on with it. He had time, when he returned to England, to look through the many volumes of his diary, and he began putting two and two together and wondering what the youngsters of that time were thinking about and doing. All the time his mind was working on a scheme, partly inspired from the pages of his diary and partly by what he saw of the way boys and girls were spending their time.

We see him now as B.-P. the Scout, the man who had taught so many men how to serve their country and be happy. We can imagine him sitting beside some quiet stream; his fishing-rod is lying on the bank beside him. He is thinking about the past, and his thoughts go back to his early days in India when 'Be Prepared' was the motto that carried him through many a difficult time. He thinks of the Guides, the men of the North-West Frontier, who taught him so much about life and self-discipline. He thinks of Africa and the making of the great road through King Prempeh's country, how he wore the famous Stetson hat, and of what a useful thing it was, along with the staff for measuring. He thinks of the little book *Aids to Scouting*, which he wrote for his Scouts of the 5th Dragoon Guards.

Then comes a picture of the African War. He smiles as he thinks of that name that they gave him—'The Wolf that Never Sleeps'. He is far too humble to think that he ever deserved it, but being so alert is a fine thing to aim at. Mafeking! His mind goes back to the day when everything seemed lost, when perhaps for the first time his heart failed him. Where is that leather bootlace? Put away in some box along with Dinizulu's necklace, and the Koodoo horn which they had given him in Matabeleland.

South African Constabulary days come into his mind. Once more the Stetson hat, the fine free-and-easy flannel shirt with the sleeves rolled up. He remembers the day when he suggested to the men that they should roll their sleeves as a sign that they were ready for anything, and when he gave them their motto, "Be Prepared".

What an adventure it had all been! Perhaps it was all to be the beginning of a much greater adventure. As usual, particularly when struck by an idea, B.-P. must start writing it down. Why not help the boys of England to be like the men of the many frontiers and outposts of the Empire where he had spent his soldiering days? It was scouting that he had taught them, scouting for men, but it would have been easier for them if they had learned it when they were boys. Why not have scouting for boys? And so he began what was to be an adventure for the whole world.

It couldn't possibly be a book with chapters—that would be too dull. Thinking, with a pen in his hand, he was once more back in India in the early days. One of his commanding officers was addressing the young subalterns of the regiment: "And when you get the men away up-country, go into their camps, sit with them round the camp fire and teach them through yarns in a friendly way. They will remember those yarns far better than what they will get in a barrack-room lecture." What an ideal Scouting for boys should be given out as camp fire yarns; and so it was. B.-P. remembered his own boyhood and the great love of adventure which had led him to become a soldier, and now that the military side of his life was nearly finished it was the scouting side that was to come into its own.

You can imagine what the boys of that time thought of it. As B.-P. himself described it: "They took to it like ducks to water!" Every boy longs for adventure. Every boy dreams of being an explorer, or a sea captain, or a great soldier, or perhaps just a pirate like Pirate Bill.

It was quite easy for B.-P. to invent the Scout uniform. The Stetson hat of his old campaigning days; the serviceable flannel shirt of the frontiersmen of all parts of the Empire; the scarf of the plainsman, which kept out dust and could be used as a bandage; the shorts, giving freedom to the legs and ventilation—and they have another advantage, for when the ground is wet you can go about without stockings, and without clammy trouser legs flapping round your ankles; the Scout staff marked with feet and inches, and the test that has to be passed before a tenderfoot may carry one. This test was based on the experience B.-P. had when in command of the party of Africans which built the great road from the coast to Kumassi in Ashanti. There is a bootlace round the hat, but you will not need telling why the bootlace is there. In the early days of scouting the hat was kept on with a leather bootlace, but every Scout should be told that that bootlace is to remind him that the darkest hour is before the dawn, and that he must show courage under all circumstances.

Here are B-P.'s own words about the Scout uniform: "The Scout uniform is very like what my men used to wear when I commanded the South African Constabulary. They knew what was comfortable, serviceable, and good protection against the weather: so Scouts have much the same uniform."

The first thing that B-P. did with the little handful of boys that he collected in order to try out the Scouting idea was to take them to camp. "No boy," he said, "is a real Scout who has never been to camp. He has missed the greatest thing of all." So even before they had uniforms B-P. took these boys to camp on an island—Brownsea Island was its name. It was very near the place where the Pirate Bill dream had happened many years before. There were sandy coves and boats for fishing. There was flag-break at early morning on a green hillside, and camp fire yarns at night under the stars with the lapping of the tide nearby. Stalking, tracking and observation, night-scouting, path-finding, despatch running, first aid, smoke signals and many other thrilling activities were practised and learned by that small handful of boys who were the first Boy Scouts.

We will leave them all listening to the story of why 'Be Prepared' was to be their motto and what that meant to the South African Constabulary. It was as a result of that camp that *Scouting for Boys* was published and scouting began to spread. Thousands of boys bought and read *Scouting for Boys*, thousands of boys became Scouts.

SCOUTING FOR GIRLS—THE GUIDES

THE early Boy Scouts, like most boys, had sisters, and many of these girls bought and read *Scouting for Boys*. They were very keen to be Boy Scouts, but as this was impossible they became Girl Scouts! Actually there was no such thing, but they invented a uniform for themselves which consisted of a Scout's hat, Scout's scarf, belt and staff. They chose whatever patrols they liked, and one of the earliest Girl Scout patrols was the Wolves. Their secret password was 'Impeesa', which, as you will remember, means 'The Wolf that Never Sleeps'. To be in the Wolf Patrol was to aim very high. I was lucky enough to be the patrol leader of the Wolves, and I am more proud of that than of anything that has happened to me since.

On the 4th September, 1909, a misty autumn day, at a place called the Crystal Palace, quite near London, the first Scout rally and conference was held. Its object was to show the public the aims and progress of the movement and how it had grown since the first Scout camp at Brownsea Island in 1907. The Crystal Palace rally was a very important occasion for the Girl Scouts, for it was there that the first band of girls were brave enough to appear in Scout uniform!

B.-P. was now called the 'Chief Scout', and the 'Chief' we will now call him to the end of this story. He was, of course, present at this rally and suddenly caught sight of the Girl Scouts. He went up to them at once, smiled at them and said: "Who are you, and what are you doing here?" I, as the patrol leader, stepped forward and saluted: "Please, Sir," I said, just a little frightened and shy, "we are the Wolf Patrol of the Girl Scouts, and we want to do Scouting like the boys." Then may have flashed through the Chief's mind these words which he has written and which have already been quoted in this book: "And there have been women scouts of the nation, too. . . . It is a grand life, but it cannot suddenly be taken up by any man or woman who thinks that they would like it; they must prepare themselves for it beforehand." Why, thought the Chief, deprive these girls of being women scouts of the future, of living this grand life. It was quite clear already that they were trying to prepare themselves by reading the camp fire yarns in *Scouting for Boys*, and carrying them out practically every day, by being Girl Scouts in the face, sometimes, of ridicule.

After that things began to happen. A little while ater I went to see the Chief at his house in London. He sat in a large armchair and talked of the days when he was soldiering in India. He told me that he was racking his brain for a name for the Girl Scouts: "The youngsters who are girls and want to do Scouting" was the way he put it. He told me of the famous regiment of Guides, of which you have already heard. Then he turned to me and said: "These men were called the Guides, and that is what I am going to call you. Do you think you can live up to it and stick to their traditions?"

As you can imagine, had it happened to you, I took it very seriously, and thinking it over afterwards realised that besides all the fun of pitching my own tent and living out of doors, cooking my own food, signalling, stalking and tracking, and wandering away across the country to seek for adventure, to find good turns to do like the knights of olden days; besides all the fun of working with my patrol, gaining badges, and making myself good at things that I found it hard to master; besides all this and so very much more there was a very serious side to being a Guide or a Scout. You had to make certain promises when you were enrolled: To be loyal to God, to help other people, to keep the Guide and Scout Law, and to do at least one good turn to somebody every day. You also had to uphold the traditions created by the men and women of the ages who have gained for themselves great honour and respect. It was upon the deeds of these countless men and women that the Chief built the traditions of Guiding and Scouting.

The first Girl Guide book was called *How Girls Can Help to Buildup the Empire*. This was written by the Chief's sister, who took a great interest in the Guide Movement. It is a splendid book, and some copies still exist. There are a great many ideas in it that are just as useful today as they were when it was written many years ago; but *Scouting for Boys* was the first great book, and anyone who tries to be a Guide or Scout without it is doomed to failure. If you read *Scouting for Boys* carefully you will see that the Chief did not invent Scouting, but that he picked out from the romantic and adventurous ideas of the world, and from its great ideals, all those things which would be most likely to help a boy or girl, a man or a woman, to run a straight race and be happy.

So the Girl Guides came into being, grew, and flourished, and no true Guide should ever be ashamed to admit that once upon a time there grew an old oak tree and the name of the tree was Scouting, and a great strong branch grew from it—and the name of the branch was Guiding. The difference between Guiding and Scouting is so slight, and the importance of Guiding and Scouting, provided that they both remain at one on all the things that really matter to them, is so vital nowadays that the nearer Guiding and Scouting, and, above all, their leaders can keep to each other the safer they will be. The Chief was talking about this once, and he said: "There is one thing that we must sweep away, and that is the slight feeling which exists among some Guides that the Scouts are not quite so efficient as they are, and the slight feeling among some Scouts that the girls are just playing at it. Guides and Scouts should never criticise each other. They should work together like the crew of a ship.

> When the crew and captain understand each other to the core,
> It takes a gale, and more than a gale, to put the ship ashore,
> For the one will do what the other commands, although they are chilled to the bone
> And both together can live through weather that neither can face alone.

"They should give each other a good name and remember that the word 'Guide' and the word 'Scout' simply means someone who goes ahead as a pioneer and adventurer, and to do this is such a busy job that we should not have time, to use a Matabele expression, 'To keep picking fleas off the other man's back'."

I wonder if the Chief, when comparing Guides and Scouts to the crew of a ship who must obey their captain implicitly in order to be safe while at sea, was thinking of that summer day long long ago when a ten-ton sailing boat was suddenly overtaken by a great storm and the boys on board only reached port safely because they obeyed, without question, the orders of their elder brother who was the skipper. The 'ship' of Guiding and Scouting has one Chief, one skipper—the boy who wished to be like Pirate Bill, and succeeded in doing it and a lot more besides!

JAMBOREE

WHEN Scouting and Guiding started the Chief had no idea that it would go beyond the British Isles, or possibly the British Empire. To use his own words: "Very gradually, like a snowball, Scouting and Guiding grew into an international movement, and like a snowball, if you go on pushing it, it will one day become so big that it cannot be pushed any further, and that will mean that every girl and boy in the world, who is keen to do so, will have a chance to become a Scout or a Guide. I want you to help me to go on pushing the snowball."

In past history there have been many movements for young people, in almost all countries, but there has never been one movement that has appealed to youngsters of so many different nationalities as Scouting. Everyone who joins must be loyal to God in his own way and must do his best to be a good citizen of his country. Both loyalty and diligence will make for happiness. The Chief always insisted that to aim at happiness was a very high aim. Here is an old English quotation that he used:

> "Doe as good Archers use, who thinking the place they intend to hit, too farre distant and knowing how farre the strength of their bow will carry, they lay their ayme a great deale higher than the mark; not for to hit so high but to bee able with the help of so high an ayme to reach the place they shoot at."

When Scouting and Guiding had spread into many countries the Chief went about visiting them, and wherever he went he told yarns. He loved to see the cheering crowds of Scouts and Guides who met him on the quaysides. He used to talk of a circle of Scouts and Guides round the world bringing happiness and friendship to each other. We are reminded of this when we see a Guide or Scout enrolled, or when we see them standing round a flagstaff for the camp prayers, or sitting round the camp fire singing or listening to a yarn. Nearly all the ceremonies in Guiding and Scouting are done in a circle. The Chief called this circle the symbol of international friendship round the world.

'Jamboree' is a funny word. It means a crowd of people having a good time, and the Chief suggested that big gatherings of Scouts should be called jamborees. The Girl Guides do not have jamborees. They have international camps, which are much the same thing. These have been held in different parts of the world. The Chief believed in these great gatherings because he knew that there could never be peace or happiness on earth until men and women learned to mix together and make friends with each other. He believed that Scouts and Guides could, by their example, lead the youth of the world in this. One of the chief purposes of the great jamborees and international camps was to draw young people together and make them appreciate each other. All rallies, world tours, jamborees and camps were held for this purpose as well as for the purpose of exchanging ideas. Perhaps in the midst of these great camps the Chief sometimes thought of the years he had spent making friends with the native peoples of Africa, which he had succeeded in doing so admirably because he treated them as such.

Once upon a time there was a lady Scoutmaster and she went for a holiday to North Africa. She was wearing a Scout badge. In the desert she met a young African. The heat was intense and he was wearing nothing but a pair of shorts held together by a Scout belt. Drawing himself up smartly he saluted her and said: "You Scout, me Scout, one Chief Scout, all world." This would be a good answer to the question: What is the meaning of Jamboree?

AUTHOR AND ARTIST

THE Chief could draw pictures and write down what he thought on paper. In the early part of his life when he was training men in the army, and later when he was training boys and girls as Scouts and Guides, he used to emphasise the usefulness of being able to draw, and by this he meant making maps and plans as well as doing quick sketches and finished pictures. He used to say that most people can draw if they try, and drawing and writing had played a big part in his own life.

He wrote a number of books when he was quite a young man, and most of these dealt with soldiering. Two particularly good ones were the *Matabele Campaign* and *Sketches in Mafeking and East Africa*. This last book was published in 1907, and is full of illustrations, many of them coloured. There are not only pictures in this book, but many sketch maps, cleverly done with a few strokes of the pen.

One of the best of all his books is a little book called *Quick Training for War*, published in 1914, and used a great deal in the army during the First World War. We read at the beginning: "Dedicated to the Young Officers and Men who have come forward in their Country's defence." This was one of the most original books on army training, and was written on a plan which the Chief called 'The Four C's of Soldiering'. The Four C's, and what the Chief has written about them, are just those things in which the Boy Scouts and the Girl Guides are training themselves at the present day. They are Courage, Commonsense, Cunning, and Cheerfulness. In *Quick Training for War* the Chief dealt with these subjects very cleverly, and long after he had written the book, when he was talking to me about it, he said: "I might re-write it now without making many alterations, and then I could call it 'Quick Training for Life'."

Scouting for Boys was the Chief's greatest book. It is a book that will never be out of date. Here is a good quotation which proves this: "The country, whose manhood has risen to the occasion as the most efficient, will take the supremacy in the peaceful campaign of commerce and industry, art and science. The worst of war is that it kills the very best of our manhood, leaving the wasters and non-efficient to carry on the national life. It is therefore our duty to take any steps we can to prevent waste of human material in the next generation." This, written very many years ago, is as true today as it ever was then. *Scouting for Boys* shows us how to prevent the waste of material to which the Chief refers. It is a book full of happy ideas and good thoughts.

The Chief loved animals, and in 1921 wrote a book entitled *An Old Wolf's Favourites—or Animals I Have Known.* In an out of the way corner of his garden he had a log cabin furnished with camp furniture and full of hunting trophies from far countries. He used to sit there and read jungle stories. On the walls of the hut were boards with lists of names on them. These were Rolls of Honour. They were the names of animals that the Chief had owned, chiefly horses and dogs, but there were also some pigs and a panther, and some of the animals' names are delightful. He gives a drawing of one of these boards in the book. Here is an extract from the introduction: "I like to have those names set up where I can read them and remind myself of the happy times we had together. You see, an animal has been made by God, just as you have been. He is therefore a fellow creature. He has not got the power of speaking our language, but he can feel pleasure or pain just as we can, and he can feel grateful to anyone who is kind to him. A Scout is always helpful to people who are crippled or blind, or deaf or dumb.

So it is up to us also to be good to those dumb creatures of ours and to make them our friends by being friends to them."

I was talking to the Chief one day about children and animals, and this is what he said: "I have never met a good man or woman who was cruel to an animal, or who disliked them, or who was indifferent to them, and have often found that a rough fellow who did not lead a particularly good life would show the best of himself with a dog or a horse. Always teach children not only to be kind to animals if they have them as pets, but to understand them, for it is quite possible for a child to be cruel to an animal through ignorance."

As has been seen in this story from the references to his diary, the Chief was very fond of writing about his adventures, and he used to tell anecdotes and different stories of things that had happened to him in all parts of the world. He never hesitated to tell a story against himself. This was typical of him, because he was completely devoid of any false pride or conceit. One of his best books of anecdotes was *Lessons from the Varsity of Life*, which is full of good pictures, done by the Chief himself. But of all the things he wrote, his diary was perhaps the best. He kept it for the whole of his life, and at his home there were many shelves full of the volumes. He once said to me, when I remarked on the number of volumes of his diary, that he did not keep it just as a habit or in order to be able to look up business matters of importance in after years, but because if he could remember all the beautiful, happy, and the solemn things that had happened to him in his life he would be a more grateful person, and a grateful person is much easier to live with. He went on to say that he used to read his old diaries and be reminded by them of some particular experience, or of particular people whom he had met and made friends with, or of people whom he had met and admired. These thoughts and remembrances gave him many happy hours. The Chief used to say that if a thing was worth enjoying, it was worth being thankful for. One day he ran across me after he had been at a performance of 'The Gang Show' by the Scouts in London. There was a song in the show called 'We've got a lot to be thankful for'. The Chief turned to me with a smile and said: "I like that song, and I like to hear all those boys singing it. I wonder if the young blighters have got any idea of how much they have got to be thankful for. But perhaps when they are as old as I am they will have got hold of the idea."

The Chief was an artist—there is no doubt about that. The word 'artist' is used here in a broad sense, because he was very musical, could play the piano and various other instruments, besides drawing and painting, which he did extremely well. He could use both hands equally well, and it has been said that once, for fun, he painted a piece of theatrical scenery with his feet. The Chief was most particular about his feet. He used to say that everyone should look after their feet as carefully as their hands. This meant, of course, that their feet should be clean, with the toe-nails looked after, and no corns. Fancy being seen painting some scenery or doing anything else for that matter, with your feet, if they were dirty! But there are other reasons for looking after your feet besides painting scenery! It is worth looking after your feet so that they do not let you down in an emergency. The Chief once did a wonderful drawing of a man being let down by his feet. Can you imagine this picture? Unfortunately it was never published.

Practically every book the Chief wrote was illustrated. He was very interested in sign writing and primitive drawings. When he was drawing a picture he used to draw it with his left hand and paint it with his right at the same time. This produced very fine results. When he wanted to bring home some special point he usually did a drawing. One of the best examples of this was the drawing of a Scout on horseback killing a dragon and underneath is written, 'The Modern St. George'.

The Chief was also a sculptor. He did one or two good busts and models—one in particular was a fine head of Captain John Smith, the explorer, who was a great hero of his, which was exhibited in the Royal Academy.

In 1935 the Chief and his family visited Franz Josef Glacier in New Zealand. There is a church there, and as usual at the east end there stands an altar. In most churches there is a reredos of some sort behind the altar with some pictures or designs of a religious nature, but behind the altar in the church of Franz Josef Glacier there is a plain glass window, and those kneeling in the church can look out at the panorama of snow-capped mountains with forests and rocks surrounding the glacier. The Chief did a beautiful drawing of this, which he sent out as his greetings card for Christmas and New Year 1935-36. In speaking about this place afterwards he said: "There was a little wooden cross on the altar and nothing else, and as you stood back in the dimness of the west end of the church you could see the dark outline of the cross against the snow. It was most beautiful, because it was most simple, and I have never forgotten it." When we think about the Chief as author and artist these words of his come back to us. He had a mind that was both beautiful and simple, and things that were both beautiful and simple always attracted him.

"WHO HATH SMELT WOODSMOKE AT TWILIGHT?"

THE Chief was a great Scout for many reasons, but mainly because he was such a good camper. He had camped all his life. As the small boy with his brothers, young Ste had wandered about the countryside of England, sleeping under the stars, cooking his own food, getting the best of fun in the world out of the life of a young backwoodsman. Throughout the campaigns in which he served in India, Africa and other parts of the world, he would have been nowhere if he had not been able to live out of doors. On many a long and strenuous trip into the wilds and jungles of foreign lands he found that it would have been impossible to be a really good and effective soldier if, to use his own words, "He had not been able to beat old Mother Nature at her own game." He always contradicted the prevalent idea that camping would mean 'roughing it'. He used to say to his men in the army, and, in later years, to the boys and girls who became Scouts and Guides: "A good Scout is never uncomfortable in camp, and if you are cold in camp wear bed socks!" Behind the tremendous knowledge which the Chief had of camping was that most valuable asset TRAINING. Here are his own words again: "Before they go to camp teach them to pitch a tent properly, to make a fire, cook a meal, and keep the place scrupulously neat and tidy, and whatever happens and whoever you are teaching, either boys or girls, keep in the background yourself and let them make their mistakes and learn by experience." What he meant by these words was that Scouts and Guides must not expect to be spoon-fed by having grown-up people doing all the work for them, and that after much practice the test of the good camper is the camp itself and what he gets out of it. At the present time people have got very far away from the Chief's idea about camping, and many boys, and even more girls, are far more content to have it all done for them than to learn by their own experiences and mistakes.

In the early days of Guiding and Scouting boys and girls made their own tents and cooking pots, ovens from old biscuit tins, and mattresses woven from heather and straw. You who read this must never be content until you can camp in the way that the Chief meant it to be done. He says that above all the value of camping is that it brings us face to face with nature, and that we should all work hard not only to enjoy the pleasures of camping, but to get our eyes wide open to the wonders of nature. When our eyes are open we shall begin to learn something of the calls and customs of animals and birds and the wonders of the stars, and the beauties of the flowers, hills and sunsets. Through all this we shall get a realisation of God the Creator. The Chief expected Guides and Scouts to do and learn all this in camp. Therefore the camping and woodcraft that he meant us to enjoy is very different from what we very often see going on in camp. Camps are frequently a sort of holiday under canvas with no very good programme running through them. This, because the patrol leaders whose responsibility it is to organise and carry through the programme in camp have forgotten or have never known what the Chief taught about camping and woodcraft. He wanted the camp to be clean, healthy and happy, a jolly place out of doors from which one went out constantly over the hills and into the woods, across the streams and down the valleys, up the lanes and over the great rolling downs, down to the sea or up to the top of the mountains. On the way there would be stalking and tracking and the following of many trails, and then in the evening back in camp each patrol would have a tale to tell at the camp fire under the stars. We picture in our minds the young officer on the North-West Frontier of India telling the yarns to his men, and the wise old General who said that those yarns would sink in further than the barrack-room lectures.

The best yarn of all will come from the patrol that has the real spirit of adventure, and has taken the trouble to find out what the Chief has taught about camping. Here are two important things that he says: "You have not finished your camp, even if you have packed up your kit and cleaned up the ground, until you have thanked the owner for the use of it and have thanked God for giving you a good time. Some people are so busy organising their camp that they have got home before they have begun to enjoy it." These last words he said just before he left England for the last time. He was afraid that we should miss the real thrill and value of camping by over-organisation, and his greatest desire was that all Guides and Scouts should really enjoy it.

You will notice that the jamborees of the Boy Scouts and the International gatherings of the Girl Guides are always held in camp. This is for a very good reason. The Chief believed that camp was a great meeting-ground for people, no matter to what country, class or creed they might belong. Scouting started in 1907 with the first camp at Brownsea Island, and the friendships formed between boys and girls of many nations in the countless camps which have been held since then cannot ever be lost. Nor can that spirit of friendship ever die, in spite of the disaster of war which may appear to overwhelm the world. The Chief never lost his faith in this friendship. Here are his own words written only a short time before he died. The greatest war in history was raging as he wrote. He sat at a small table on the verandah of his African home:

"The darkest hour is before the dawn, the blackest cloud can only shade for a time the blue sky and sunshine which is there above it. One thing is essential for general and permanent peace, and that is a total change of spirit among the peoples. The change to closer mutual understanding, to the subjugation of national prejudices and the ability to see with the other fellow's eye in friendly sympathy."

There is no place where you can better "see with the other fellow's eye in friendly sympathy" than in CAMP. The Chief hoped that there would be no Guide or Scout who could say, when starting out on the adventure of being grown up: "I was a Guide or Scout, but I never went to camp."

Who hath smelt woodsmoke at twilight? Who
Hath heard the birch-log burning?
Who is quick to read the noises of the night?
Let him follow with the others
For the young men's feet are turning
To the camps of proved desire and known delight!

CAMP FIRE YARNS

THE Chief, like many good scouts and backwoodsmen, could tell a good yarn. He was able to produce, at short notice, some excellent and telling short story. No story of him as a scout would be complete without quoting some of these anecdotes. Here are one or two:

"An Englishman wanted to fight a duel with a Red Indian. The Indian smiled and said that he would fight, but that the Englishman would get the worst of it. When asked his reasons for saying this he said that he noticed that the Englishman always kept his mouth half open. The Red Indian had no fear whatever of a man who would do this because it was the sign of a weak character."

The Chief was anxious that Scouts and Guides should keep themselves fit and healthy. "It seemed a terrible thing," he said, "to think that if you added up all the working hours that men lose in Great Britain through ill health it would amount to something over twenty million weeks, and half the time this loss of wages, trade, etc., is the fault of the workers themselves. Just imagine an engine driver and all the care that he takes to keep his machinery in good order! How clean, properly lubricated and carefully used the engine must be in order that it may work smoothly and efficiently! But the human body is a machine much more wonderful than any man-made engine, and it needs far more attention and better understanding if it is to be kept well. Most important of all, people can, by taking care of their own body, improve it and make it bigger and stronger, which is more than any engineer can do with his engine!"

The Chief was once asked by a high authority on education whether he thought that large sums of money should be collected, or given by the Government, to erect gymnasia in every town all over the country. This man thought that it would be money well spent because it would develop health and strength. The Chief's answer to this suggestion was that the two strongest and healthiest races he had ever known were the Zulus of Africa and the Bhutani peasants of the Himalayas, and that in neither country had he ever noticed a gymnasium! There was plenty of God's fresh air and lots of walking and running and climbing to be done in the daily work of these people, and the Chief believed that these were good enough tonics for any man.

He never tired of telling yarns about what he called the joy of the open road. To use his own words: "Something that costs you nothing and is more valuable than anything that money can buy." There is no pleasure that comes near to the joy of cooking your own food on an open fire, with the scent of the woodsmoke as it curls up amongst the branches overhead. This is a good and wholesome thing at the end of a long day under the sky. The Scout or Guide who is really keen on woodcraft has discovered the secret heart of the movement and has captured something which will be with them for ever.

The Chief was on a fishing expedition in one of those lovely counties in the Midlands of England where streams wander through the woods and there are perfect places for sleeping under the stars. He took out his notebook, which he always carried with him, and here are a few things that he wrote in it during that summer week-end. These notes were destined to be used long afterwards in a camp fire yarn which he wrote for Rover Scouts: "There is no view like that from your lair on the woodland hillside. And there is no sleep like that in the open with a warm blanket beneath you. More under than above you is the tramp's secret for lying warm at nights. The sound of the night and the companionship of the beasts and birds make you feel a comrade of them all. Rain? Cold? Yes, I suppose they come, but you really get to disregard them when you are in the regular swing and habit of week-end camping."

The daily good turn is one of the principles on which Scouting and Guiding are built. In his yarns the Chief was constantly reminding boys and girls of this, and that they must keep their eyes open in order to see what was needed to be done. Here is a good yarn to tell at a camp fire. It is really the story of a man who had a guilty conscience: "Two men were sitting in a bus. One sat with his eyes tightly closed. His friend whispered that people were staring at him, and suggested that he should open his eyes. This he refused to do, and when they got out at their destination his friend asked him why he made himself look so ridiculous. His rather sheepish reply was: 'I sit in the bus with my eyes shut, old chap, because I can't bear to see all the women standing'."

The Chief was constantly bringing into his yarns the importance of respecting one's parents. He said that a large proportion of the men who had risen to eminence in the world owed very much of their character and success to the influence of their mothers. A man cannot fully repay this debt. She has given her best for him. The best he can do is to show that he is grateful by proving himself to be a good man. Sir Thomas Lipton once told the Chief that when he was a small boy he realised how tremendously happy he had made his mother by bringing her his first week's wages. "Why, Thomas," she said, "you will be getting me a carriage and pair next!" Sir Thomas went on to say that this remark of his mother's caught his imagination, and thus he developed his great ambition. His whole effort was then devoted to the one aim of making enough money to buy a carriage and pair as a surprise offering to his mother. He told the Chief later that among the many exciting incidents of his life the proudest and happiest of all was when he was able to hand over the prize that he had gained for her. Commenting upon Sir Thomas Lipton's words, the Chief said: "So, in making your way to success, remember that your progress will not merely be a satisfaction to yourself, but to those who love you, and most of all perhaps to your mother. When difficulties and temptations come along, turn your thoughts to those who loved and cared for you when you were young. Think what their wish for you would be, then act upon it, and with the grace of God it will help you through life."

The Chief used to say that the yarn at the camp fire on a Sunday night in camp should be a different sort of yarn from the week-day one. A lot of people are very much afraid of religion, and some think it is a sign of weakness to believe in such things, but the Chief thought that religion was essential to happiness, and he said that if Scouts and Guides were really out to make their way to success, i.e. happiness, they must "avoid being sucked in by irreligious humbugs, and have a religious basis to their lives". The Chief recommended three ways of doing this. Here are his own words: "Say your prayers regularly, read that wonderful old book, the Bible, and read that other wonderful old book, the Book of Nature, and see and study all that you can of the wonders and beauties that nature provides for your enjoyment. Then turn your mind to how you can best serve God while you still have the life that He has lent you."

Many people who live in towns are never able to realise the beauty of nature because they seldom see it. Their eyes are more trained to look at shops, advertisements, other people, and 'Safety First'. But those who have lived with nature and have caught the wonder of it, can, when they come to a town, catch glimpses of it even in the dingy streets. Again, he tells us: "At one time in my life I had to cross Westminster Bridge every day—at sunrise and again at sunset—and scarcely a day passed when I didn't find myself standing to gaze at the scene with immense pleasure."

The first half of the first Guide and Scout Promise may often be brought into camp fire yarns, especially on a Sunday evening, and here are a few simple quotations from different sources, used by the Chief, that will give some ideas of what to think about on these occasions:

"How many observe Christ's birthday, how few His precepts! It is easier to keep holidays than the Commandments."

"I can see how it might be possible for a man to look down upon earth and be an atheist, but I do not see how he can look up into the heavens by night and say there is no God."

> And nature the old nurse took
> The child upon her knee
> Saying, here is the story-book
> The Father has written for thee.
>
> Come wander with me, she said,
> Into regions yet untrod
> And read what is still unread
> In the manuscript of God.

The Chief was the master-teller of camp fire yarns, and just before leaving England for the last time he expressed, as one of his greatest desires, that camp fire yarns and the telling of them should never die out in the Guide and Scout movements. "It takes some courage to tell a yarn," he would say, "and we British are a reserved people and don't always like to talk about the things that mean most to us, but a good story fires the imagination and is often a source of inspiration to those who may hear it. And I have heard many a good yarn told, not by grown-ups at all, but by the youngsters themselves."

LADIES AND GENTLEMEN

ONE day the Chief was asked to define the meaning of the words 'lady' and 'gentleman'. He answered the question by telling this story: "I was talking to some Scouts in camp and asking them some questions about different things. They were senior boys, and I thought it was time to think about growing up. Some of them were about to go to work. So I said, 'I want you chaps to tell me—what are the things that make a lady or gentleman?' The answer came at once from a fellow sitting in front. 'Please, Sir, a lady or a gentleman is someone who has got a lot of money and a good position.' As you may imagine this gave me rather a shock, and I wondered how many other young people thought the same thing. However, on another occasion I was talking to some boys from a poor part of a big city, and I asked them the same question, and one of them answered with these words: 'A gentleman is a bloke wat keeps even his toe-nails clean'."

That is exactly what the Chief always said, only, of course, using different words! A lady or gentleman is someone who has a clean outlook about life. They may be rich or poor, young or old, it does not matter. Riches, position, power, mean nothing at all. In speaking of his men on one occasion in the army when he had been in a very tight corner and the battle was over and won, the Chief said: "They are just the fellows to be with whether you are fighting alongside them in war or training them in peace-time, because they are gentlemen right through."

There is a quiet spot in the county of Hampshire where green meadows and little lovely woods full of primroses in springtime make the place seem England heart and soul. This was home to the Chief. The name of his house was Pax Hill—the Hill of Peace—where he found peace after journeyings in many lands, and where he shared the peace with a family that was very dear to him. One day the Guide company in which I was a patrol leader had the privilege of camping there. We had been in the woods and fields all day, and at evening we returned to have supper and camp fire at the foot of the Hill of Peace. Out came the Chief, with a couple of dogs at his heel, and a welcoming smile for everyone. Many songs were sung, and then camp prayers. Before we dispersed the Chief came up and said: "I love that last song best of all. It's my favourite." This is the first verse of the song:

> There is a lady sweet and kind,
> And never face so pleased my mind.
> I did but see her passing by,
> And yet I love her till I die.

It happened many years before that when the Chief was walking in the Park at Knightsbridge, a girl passed him and walked ahead, crossing the road with a swinging stride. He did not see her face. Two years later he was starting on his first world tour visiting Scouts in many lands, and as the passengers came aboard one of them, a young woman, walked the deck in front of him. The same walk, the same swinging stride. The Chief had a good memory—Knightsbridge. And by the time he had finished his world tour he was engaged to marry this gracious lady. Perhaps that was the memory at that camp fire—who knows? But anyhow, that is how the Girl Guides got a Chief Guide.

Here are some of the things the Chief said, and how well they apply to us at the present day:

" 'A London crowd is exceptionally well-mannered. It will stand for hours and watch in silence a large safe being hauled up to the top of a high building. In silence, mind you, without offering a word of advice to the men at the job! A great example of self-control.' That is what Pett Ridge has to say on self-control and how it contributes to good manners. Old William of Wickham declared long ago that manners maketh the man, and he was right. A gentleman is gentle and courteous—that is, he shows deference, human sympathy and unbreakable good humour. It makes him a gentleman, and I have seen it very truly said that it is just as hard for a duke as a bricklayer to be a gentleman. The same thing applies to women and to the making of a lady. I used to play polo against a certain team who had one very good back player, but he had his weak spot—he was not a gentleman, he had a bad temper, so one only had to bump into him and he lost his temper and was perfectly useless to his side. It is much the same in a discussion. If your adversary cannot control his temper you have him at your mercy—that is, if you can control your own. Remember this. If you are in the right there is no need to lose your temper. If you are in the wrong you can't afford to. Go ahead on that. Behave like a gentleman or a lady. With politeness and self-control you will win every time."

ENDURANCE

THERE was a word the Chief was very fond of using when referring to the high qualities required of and possessed by the sort of men he had worked with in the course of his army career. He would say: "It is the STICKABILITY of the man that really counts." And by this he did not only mean the power to put up with hardship and the strength of body to knock down an adversary in fair fight, he meant an all-round sort of fellow who, after years of practice of a good many different things, had become physically, mentally and spiritually strong. Thus, when his moment came when everything depended on his all-round strength, he was able to stand up to things and, more important still, not to let other people down through his own weakness.

Here is what the Chief said about endurance: "Since most cases of physical decay are preventable, they open for instructors a field for doing a work of national value.

Boys and girls should be taught to be personally responsible for their own health, strength and sanitary surroundings. . . . One motto of a Scout is: 'Never say die till you are dead', and if he acts up to this it will pull him out of many a bad place when everything seems to be going wrong for him. It means that mixture of pluck, patience and strength which we call Endurance."

There was a famous scout called Colonel Selous, and he gave a good example of a scout's endurance. When on one of his African expeditions he had many and dangerous adventures, and none but a scout with extraordinary endurance could have lived through them. Selous was a man who as a lad had made himself strong by care and exercise. He neither drank nor smoked, and he kept up his pluck all the time. The Chief himself showed all these qualities throughout his long life. He used to say, quite rightly, that if you want to enjoy great adventures when you are a man or woman: "You must not be a 'slopper' when you are young. You must train yourself up to be strong, healthy and active." The word 'slopper' is a nasty word, but unfortunately it describes a great many people of our own time, and they are never healthy people in body or mind. It is interesting to note that in talking or writing about Endurance the Chief is always giving good advice about how to look after different parts of the body—nose, ears, teeth, nails, hair, etc., and, in a more general way, how to keep healthy by being clean in body and mind and not doing anything to excess, such as smoking, eating and drinking.

The Chief was a great believer in the old motto: 'Early to bed, early to rise, makes a man healthy, wealthy and wise.' Sometimes it takes a certain amount of determination to go to bed early and to keep it up, but even more so, to get up early, and do that regularly. Test out your body and be sure that you are master of it and that it is not master of you. See how far you can walk without getting tired. The Chief used to do this when he was a boy, and on long expeditions in the army, when in the saddle for many hours on end, it was a real test of endurance. But whatever kind of endurance tests you give yourself, bring yourself up to scratch gradually, and if you find a thing is really too much for you never overdo it.

The Chief arrived at Foxlease one day with a parcel under his arm. It turned out to be a framed copy of the Guide Law beautifully written out in script by himself. Directly he had unpacked it everyone noticed that there were eleven instead of ten Guide Laws written out. The eleventh was 'A Guide is not a fool.' He used to say the same with Scouts, too. I asked him what made him think of adding this law, and he said: "First, because it is a good one and makes you pull yourself together and think when you are about to do something stupid; and, secondly, because I once saw a lot of Guides in the pouring rain without coats and they told me they were hardening themselves off! To be hardy is a good thing, to be foolhardy is no good at all!"

Test out your mind. Many people have a bad memory and bad powers of observation. They just wander through life like blind bats, and have a very dull time in consequence. The Chief used to test out his men in the army by playing Kim's game with them. He once had a soldier servant who was a splendid fellow in every way, but had a bad memory. This was very tiresome for himself and for everyone else. He was sent away to another unit for a time, but eventually came back after a period of three years. The Chief noticed at once that he was far more alert and had a much better memory than when he was with him before. He asked him how he had managed it, and the answer was: "Well, Sir, it was like this: I've got my ambition, and you once said a long time ago that no soldier with a bad memory could get very far, so I started training myself, and every time I had a lapse of memory I was pretty hard on myself in one way or another, and that seemed to have helped matters."

The Chief, however, was not content with endurance of body and mind only; he constantly used the expression, 'having the right spirit'. Training your spirit is a tougher task than training body or mind. Here is a good story told by the Chief to illustrate this. He calls this story 'Alone in the Andes':

"I started out alone before dawn one morning in the Andes of South America to climb a mountain-side. The chill gloom of the early dawn was deepened by the depth of the canyon in which I started, and the heights loomed round one against the sky, but in the darkness it was difficult to judge of their height or distance. As I climbed the ascent before me the light gradually opened out, and cliffs and rock-masses stood up more clearly defined. The air was very cold and clear and still, and the great, tense silence around one seemed to press itself upon me. Not a murmur of a brook, not a chirp of birds, not a whisper of a breeze. Stillness everywhere. Yet it did not seem altogether a dead stillness. It seemed rather as if everything—the mountains, the valleys, the peaks and the boulders—were all standing at attention waiting, looking for the coming day. It seemed almost sacrilegious to break that silence with the clicking of one's footsteps among the stones. I climbed higher and higher, and breathing became more difficult, while the sense of loneliness and smallness grew upon me in that intense silence and among those vast gables of the roof of the world. And as one looked around, peak after peak took up the rosy radiance of the dawn.

"I stumbled on, awed almost to horror by it all, when, at the moment just when I most needed some touch with the human world, over the next rise there stood up before me a figure—the figure of 'Christ the Redeemer' . . . a fine statue happily placed for its purpose of marking the boundary, and a sign of perpetual peace between the States of Argentine and Chile. But even more happily placed than its sculptor had designed in giving, at that spot, a tangible link between the human and Divine, the link which Christ in His time had come on earth to give."

In this story we have a perfect combination of the three things which constitute endurance. The Chief climbing a mountain-side, steep and rocky and requiring bodily strength in order that the climb might be accomplished. As he climbs he is thinking, he is allowing his mind to become full of the beauty of his surroundings, as he looks round and sees peak after peak taking up the rosy colours of the dawn. It takes some endurance of mind to appreciate beauty while the body is struggling to accomplish the great effort. And then he sees the figure of 'Christ the Redeemer' who gives us the spirit which will enable us to endure all things of body and mind. Endurance of spirit is really being able to appreciate the holy things of life, and there is no doubt that prayer, which the Chief believed in tremendously, needs an enormous amount of earnest application and determination.

No story of the Chief is complete without reference to his tremendous powers of endurance and to the health of body, mind and spirit which radiated from him. There was an old English poet called Dryden who wrote:

Better to hunt in fields for health unbought
Than fee the doctor for a nauseous draught:
The wise, for cure, on exercise depend;
God never made his work for man to mend.

The Chief was quoting this one day to a big gathering of Scouts, and he finished his yarn with these words: "So all you fellows who are learning to be Scouts and learning to be the men of the future, see to it that you don't have to take a lot of nasty medicine in order to keep fit, that you take plenty of exercise, which is far better than any medicine, and that you remember that a good Scout keeps himself fit, not only in order that he may be able to enjoy himself but, far more important than this, in order that he may be prepared to help other people when the opportunity arises. Stickability is what you want, and I advise you to write the word out and stick it up somewhere where you can see it every day; and good luck to you!"

FLEUR-DE-LYS

In the early days of Scouting, as indeed has happened a great many times since, certain critics accused the Chief of making the movement military. Here are the Chief's own words about this: "Whenever anything new is started there are bound to be people who get up on their hind legs to find fault with it, often before they know what it is all about. In this case they said that the Scout Movement was designed to teach boys how to be soldiers, and they quoted in proof that the crest of the movement was, as they described it, a spearhead, the emblem of battle and bloodshed. I was asked by cable what I had to say about it. I telegraphed back: 'The crest is the Fleur-de-Lys—a lily, the emblem of peace and purity'." The Fleur-de-Lys has come to be the sign of the Scouts in almost every country in the world.

The badge of the Girl Guides has a very similar meaning, and the Girl Guide Movement is no more military than the Boy Scouts. Both Guide and Scout badges, with their three points and three leaves, represent the Three Promises: Duty to God; Helpfulness to Others; Obedience to the Law. Guiding and Scouting are full of emblems and badges, symbols that represent the training that is given in the movement. All this training is arranged under four headings, and the Chief used to say to patrol leaders and others that they ought to work out all the training that they gave under these four headings:

Intelligence: How much of Guiding and Scouting can be put under this heading. All the things that make a Guide or Scout quicker on the uptake; all the badges and tests that make them more on the spot. The Chief used to say about it: "Don't be content to be a dud, be alert, be prepared, and if anyone asks what you should be prepared for, the answer should be 'For anything'."

Handcraft: The Chief gave excellent yarns about the ideals of our movement. But he was also a practical man, and showed Scouts and Guides how to make things with their hands. He thought that boys and girls should be ashamed if they could not mend their own clothes; do anything that was needed about the house, and, especially with reference to the Guides, he said: "I do not like the idea of a girl being of no use with her hands. A woman's job is to be neat and useful with her fingers, and she should take pride in cooking, sewing, washing and general housework, turning things out in an orderly and finished way." Another important handcraft is knotting. The Chief tells us that a knot should be tied with stout cord or rope. Always have the real thing to practise with. But perhaps the most thrilling thing of all is fire-making. The Chief held that it was a great art to be able to make a fire properly. You must learn to lay a fire with damp wood as well as dry, and to make many difficult types of fires. The very word 'handcraft' means to be careful and accurate.

HEALTH: We often see the slogan 'Fitness Wins' written in books and magazines. This is certainly true, and the healthy Guide or Scout is the one who will find that peace and purity which the Chief speaks of in describing the Fleur-de-Lys or Scout Badge. A person with no health of mind has no peace and has not found out the meaning of the Tenth Law.

SERVICE: Can you keep your head in an emergency? If you have had no experience you must try and stage some emergency, or get someone to spring one on you and see what happens. Could you render first aid if someone was bleeding seriously, suffering from shock or severe burns? Can you use a public telephone? Can you remember, and pass on accurately, a verbal message? There are many, many other questions that Guides and Scouts should ask themselves, and not only ask, but be able to answer, so that when the moment arrives for them to render service they may be able to do so accurately and well.

Proficiency Badges are important emblems of our movement. They are the outward sign to show the general public what we can do—not in order that the general public may give us a pat on the back, but in order that they may ask our help. So you see that it is very important that Guides and Scouts should not get badges when they do not really deserve them. Examiners are very kind people, and the Chief used to deplore this fact, because he said that they were not nearly strict enough. This is very often the case. The Chief gained many Proficiency Badges during his soldiering days, and he always made things as hard as possible for himself, and then as hard as possible for his men. The word 'badge' means an emblem, and an emblem in the olden days was the sign or symbol carried by a knight to show that he had won a hard battle with himself. All Proficiency Badges in the Guide and Scout Movement must be looked upon in this way, if they are to be of any value at all.

Once upon a time there was a band of knights who lived in a castle, and every squire in the band, before he was knighted, was given a silver shield without a device. They had to keep their shields bright, as no design was upon them. When they had done something—in other words, when they had tested themselves sufficiently and done some deed or passed some test of real merit—a silver star would appear miraculously upon their shield. This was a sign that they could be knighted. They had to do some practical good and pass some practical test. They also had to discipline themselves in mind and body. Every Guide and Scout has an imaginary shield when they are enrolled. Then comes the time of testing with Tenderfoot, Second Class and First Class, Proficiency Badges, and much more besides. So they all have the opportunity to train and test themselves. The Chief was fond of this story of the knights. He used to say that Guides and Scouts should aim at getting a device on their shield. Perhaps his own device is the flower of the Lily.

THE GOLDEN ARROW

The story of B.-P. the Scout would fill many volumes, but only a few chapters can be given to it in this little book. You can see, when you read this story, that the Chief entered into Scouting himself and made it part of his life. He was a Scout from the earliest days, when we meet him as a boy lying on the sand one summer's day, or in camp on Brownsea Island in 1907, until the time when Scouting became world wide. It is an undoubted fact that although the whole of Scouting and all its activities were a precious source of happiness to the Chief, it was the world-wide brotherhood of Scouting that appealed to him most. The outstanding fact is that Scouting knows no distinction of country, class or creed, and that no matter to what country, class or creed, men or women, boys or girls, may belong, theirs may be the gift of the brotherhood of Scouts and the sisterhood of Guides which the Chief gave to the world. This message was interpreted by the great jamborees and international gatherings, and it had many symbols. The greatest of all, and perhaps dearest to the Chief, was the Golden Arrow. He said of it, at the World Jamboree at Arrowe Park in 1929: "My brothers, you will remember how the Golden Arrow has been handed out to each country as a symbol of the goodwill flying forth to all the ends of the earth through the brotherhood of Scouting. You know the old lines:

> I shot an arrow into the air,
> It fell to earth I know not where.

"That is the story of the Golden Arrow of Scouting, and every time we carry out the Scout Law in our lives and spread goodwill and fellowship round the world through the brotherhood of Scouts, we do not know where it may fall."

Writing later from Africa, when he was ill and going gently to his last days, he said: "Though the war may have killed very many of our dear comrades and companions, it has not killed all, and it has not killed the spirit. You . . . who still live, can carry on that same spirit and will develop it with all the greater force when you realise that you are taking up the torch which was dropped by those who have been struck down. Few of those comrades of ours could have foreseen that within a short time they would have been fighting and giving their lives for their country. But we do know that through being prepared as Scouts they were the better able to face their fate with courage and good cheer. As your tribute to their memory it is open to you to make goodwill and friendship for brother Scouts at home and abroad. This must be your aim more directly than ever before."

In the early part of the Second World War a Polish soldier was taken prisoner in his own country and managed to escape. He was a Scout, and had been the one to receive the Golden Arrow from the hands of the Chief at the Jamboree at Arrowe Park on the coming-of-age of Scouting in 1929. He had lost everything—home, family, and all that he held most dear—except one precious possession—the Golden Arrow, in rough wood, which he was determined to take away with him. After passing through many adventures he reached Great Britain. Nothing arrived except one brave worn-out Polish soldier and his Golden Arrow. He sought out a Scout whom he knew, and by whom he had been taught his Scouting in the old days at Gilwell Park. To him he gave the Arrow, saying that for the present it was no longer of any use to him. He had brought it to the only haven he knew. It was afterwards given into the safe keeping of a small country troop, who looked upon it with great pride. The Chief never knew this story, but would have loved it if he had, and might truly have said:

> I shot an arrow into the air,
> It fell to earth I know not where.

Some day, when war is over and peace has come, the

Arrow will go back to Poland. That is what the brotherhood of Scouts does for people. That is the spirit of Scouting. And badly will that spirit of comradeship be needed for the reconstruction of the world that lies ahead.

B.-P. the Scout was tremendously keen on the idea that young people should prepare for the future and look forward to the days ahead of them when they might be leaders in the world. He always looked forward himself into the future with gallant and high-hearted happiness—and there we will leave B.-P. the Scout, the hero of many a boy and girl.

PART IV

THE MAN

EVENING

"I WILL have the poor people to be as rich as we are, and they ought by rights to be as happy as we are. You must pray to God whenever you can. But you cannot be good with only praying; you must try to be very good." These words are written under the heading: "Laws for me when I am old", by R. S. S. Baden-Powell, just after his eighth birthday. After his eightieth birthday he wrote: "I have had a most happy life, and I want each of you to have as happy a life, too. You will find that heaven is not a kind of happiness somewhere up in the skies after you are dead, but right here and now in this world." This last message was written to the many children, boys and girls, Scouts and Guides, whom the Chief loved so well, and this message undoubtedly shows that what the boy B.-P. wrote when he was eight years of age was carried out by him throughout life. No one can come to the end of a long life and be completely happy unless he has learnt to be loyal to God, to help other people whether they are rich or poor, and to have some law in his life which he can live up to.

This book is only one of many stories that have been written about this great man, Baden-Powell of Gilwell.

He trained boys and girls to become the right sort of men and women, and the reason why his training carried so much weight was because he trained himself first in such things as alertness, common sense, healthiness, discipline and the great art of good comradeship. Last, but not least, he was always ready for and never afraid of responsibility. The boy or girl who wants to be a great man or woman—and most of them do in their inmost heart—must follow the teaching of B.-P. the man, who was before all things a Christian and a gentleman.

This is a big statement to make about anyone, and when youngsters today think their thoughts about the future—What am I going to be in life? What am I going to see in life? Where am I going to go in life? What am I going to do in life?—they must qualify all the answers to these questions by saying that whatever life may bring to them they will first strive to make the world a better place for other people to live in.

There came a day when B.-P., an old man, brave and young in heart, went round some of his favourite haunts in England for the last time. He had planned to go to Africa to live the last years of his life, and his plan was made gently and with dignity. He made no outcry as many do at the end of life. He never said those sad words one sometimes hears: "I hate to get old." He visited his friends, and above all he visited the places he loved. Age meant nothing to him except, perhaps, as a happy time of resting in quiet, when he could look back upon the road along which he had travelled and think of the glad days that were past and of all the joys and adventures that he had experienced.

Just at this time, when he was preparing this last stage, as he always prepared carefully every stage of his life as far as possible, he wrote: "There was a will in the paper the other day in which the man who made it spoke of a happy, successful life in these words: 'Finally, I should like to place on record that I have been one of God's luckiest creatures, and I can only wish I could have been more worthy of the affection lavished on me by my mother, father, brothers, wife, relations and others. I have had a wonderfully happy time, and I thank God for the boon of life.' " The Chief went on to say that this man had left only £128 behind him, but that he was rich in being happy.

About the same time the Chief wrote: "My old headmaster, Dr. Haig-Brown, wrote this verse, giving his recipe for a long life and a happy one:

> A diet moderate and spare;
> Freedom from base financial care;
> Abundant work and little leisure;
> A love of beauty more than pleasure.
> An even and contented mind
> In charity with all mankind.
> Some thoughts too sacred for display
> In the broad light of common day.
> A peaceful home, a loving wife;
> Children, who are the crown of life.
> This lengthens out the years of man
> Beyond the psalmist's narrow span.

B.-P. loved these words, and often quoted them, adding: "True content comes to those who can look back on past doings with a clear conscience and who love their work. Be content with what you have got, not with what you would like to have; this is a great step to happiness. There is another thing: a sense of humour is indispensable if you are to make your way successfully in life. There is no use in going through life with a hang-dog expression on your face. There are lots of young people who set themselves up as cynics with a sort of superior contentment. Cynics have no sense of humour, and contentment is after all only a step towards happiness. Happiness cannot be complete without active love and service for others. Otherwise it would only be just a selfish state of mind."

Thus the Chief journeyed towards the evening of his life, and as so often happens at evening, the storms were past, the wind dropped, and there was a great calm. A friend of mine in speaking of him at the time said: "I only met him a few times in late years, but he was a dear old man, so young in heart."

TOMORROW

THE day came when B.-P. went to visit Gilwell Park for the last time. This was his last Reunion. The Scout training centre in the heart of Epping Forest had been the scene for him of many gatherings, camp fires and conferences, where men and women, boys and girls from all over the world had gathered to learn how to become good Scouts. Many a yarn the Chief had given them there, and on that last visit we see him one evening walking under the trees with a Scout friend and his dog at his heel. He is talking in that quiet voice of his, which always had a touch of humour and good fellowship about it: "For my part I have given myself three more years to go, and that makes me hurry up and get things done, and get all the enjoyment I can out of life, because in three years it will be too late. I have always given myself three years, because it is a very good incentive, and some day it will come true. In the meantime it makes you bust along and get all you can out of life, and," he added quietly, with a very cheerful smile, "it will be up to the youngsters to keep Guiding and Scouting going. Tomorrow will be their day. They must do it with all the will that is in them, and the old ones, like you and me, must just sit back and let them have their chance."

How true these words have been proved to be during these last years! Thousands of the older folk have been called to national service since the war, and Scouting and Guiding has had to be carried on chiefly by the initiative and enthusiasm of the patrol leader.

B.-P. the man, at the end of his long and happy life, was content to sit back and give his blessing to the young ones. He wanted them to have this chance. So if you are one of the older ones who is reading this story, don't be afraid to follow the example of the Chief and sit back and give the younger ones their chance. And if you are one of the youngsters reading this story, make sure that when your chance of leadership comes you will be prepared to take it and use it. But, old or young, you will have to acquire that great virtue of humility which the Chief possessed in such overwhelming measure and which he maintained was the keynote to happiness and success.

In 1934 the Chief wrote a Foreword to a very humble book of poems that I had written, and later, when commenting on the book, he said that his favourite verse therein was on the subject of growing old:

> And when I am old and glad with age,
> Because of the power in me
> That comes from loving such lovely things
> As mountains and hills and the sea,
> I will lay me down and take my rest
> And peace shall abide with me.

"I like to think," he said, "of growing old bravely and happily." He spoke much of his children and grandchildren and of his love for them, and of how much home life and all the little intimate things that take place in a happy home meant to him. Helping in the house, feeding his dogs, tidying up the garden, caring for the trees, and coming in at evening to the firelight and the sound of happy voices meant everything to him; the scent of the garden on a summer night, the birds coming home at evening, and the sense of comradeship with those whom he loved. At the end of one of the last books that he wrote he quoted some favourite lines of his:

> Sleep after toyle, port after stormie seas,
> Ease after warre, death after life, doth greatly please.

And that is undoubtedly what he felt at the end of his full life. He had a wonderful faculty for seeing, appreciating, and absorbing beauty. He was "without fear and without reproach"—Baden-Powell the Man, Chief Scout of the World, and a very gentle knight.

But this story has no end because "Tomorrow is their day".

THE TRAIL

1857 Born at 6 Stanhope Street, London, W.

1869 Won scholarship for Fettes from Rose Hill, Tunbridge Wells. Also obtained a nomination for Charterhouse, so in either case a free education was assured.

1870 Went to Charterhouse as Gownboy Foundationer.

1873 Moved with school from London to new Charterhouse at Godalming.

1876 VI Form. In Football and Rifle Team for two years. Left Charterhouse for Oxford (unattached). Passed Army Exam., 2nd for Cavalry, 4th for Infantry. Direct Commission (without Sandhurst) to 13th Hussars. Joined the Regiment at Lucknow as sub-lieutenant.

1877 Garrison Course of eight months at Lucknow for Lieutenant.

1878 Passed 1st Class with 'extra' Certificate for reconnaissance.
Commission ante-dated. (Thus gained between two and three years' seniority over men who passed the same entrance exam. in 1876, who had to go to Sandhurst.)

1879 Home on sick-leave.
Went through Musketry Instruction course at Hythe. Passed 1st class with 'extra' Certificate.

1880 Rejoined 13th Hussars in India and accompanied the Regiment to Afghanistan (Kandahar) with General Phayre's force, Colonel (Sir) Baker Russell commanding the 13th Hussars.
Employed making maps of the Battlefield of Maiwand for use at the court-martial on officers concerned in the defeat there.

1881 Regiment moved to Quetta. Shot himself in leg *en route* during night raid at the Kojak Pass.

1882 Regiment marched through North India, nine hundred miles, to Muttra.
Appointed Musketry Instructor to Regiment.

1883 At Muttra. Won Kadir Cup—Pigsticking Challenge Cup.
Temporarily attached to staff of Duke of Connaught at Meerut.
Appointed Adjutant. Promoted Captain.

1884 Regiment moved from Muttra to Natal to assist if necessary in co-operation with Sir Charles Warren's expedition to Bechuanaland.
Carried out secret reconnaissance of Natal frontier of six hundred miles.
Went on big game shooting expedition in Portuguese East Africa at Inhambane.
Published *Reconnaissance and Scouting*.

1885 Regiment returned home to Norwich.
Moved to Colchester.
Resigned Adjutancy.

1886 Regiment moved to Manchester, B.-P.'s squadron to Liverpool (Seaforth).
Wrote *Cavalry Instruction*.

1887 Appointed A.D.C. to G.O.C. South Africa, General H. A. Smyth.

1888 Campaign in Zululand against Dinizulu.
Acted as Military Secretary and as Intelligence Officer to Flying Column.
Confirmed as Military Secretary.
Promoted Brevet-Major.

1889 Home on sick-leave.
Returned to South Africa and appointed Secretary to Commission to Swaziland under Sir F. de Winton jointly with Boer Commission.
Sir H. A. Smyth appointed Acting Governor Cape Colony, B.-P. became automatically Acting Military Secretary to Governor. Published *Pigsticking or Hog Hunting*.

1890 Transferred to Malta with Sir H. A. Smyth (Governor of Malta) as Military Secretary.
Published *Vedette*.

1891 Appointed Intelligence Officer for Mediterranean—as such visited surrounding countries—Italy, Albania, Greece, Turkey, Tunis, Algeria, etc.

1892 Visited Bosnia and Herzgovina, also Austrian and Italian manoeuvres. Visited Montenegro.

1893 Resigned as Military Secretary, Malta. Visited Tunisia and Algeria. Rejoined 13th Hussars in Ireland—Cork and Ballincollig. Manoeuvres at Curragh.

1894 Regiment at Dundalk.
Manoeuvres at Churn, Berks. Brigade-Major to General French, Douglas Haig being his A.D.C.

1895 Commanded Squadron at Belfast.
Ashanti Expedition. West Africa. Raised and commanded local recruits to Kimassu.
Brevet Lt.-Col. and Medal.

1896 Matabele Expedition, South Africa. Appointed Chief Staff Officer to G.O.C. Sir F. Carrington.
Carried out Scouting in Matopo Hills.
Commanded Column clearing country on Shangani, Belingine, etc., seven hundred miles.
Moved to Mashonaland.
Published *The Downfall of Prempeh.*

1897 End of Matabele campaign. Brevet-Colonel and Medal.
Returned home with Cecil Rhodes.
Rejoined 13th Hussars in Dublin as Squadron-Commander.
Appointed to command 5th Dragoon Guards in India and joined them at Meerut.
Published *The Matabele Campaign.*

1898 Commanded Brigade of Cavalry for manoeuvres.
Visited troops at the front attacking Tochi Pass under General Bindon Blood.
Tiger shooting trip to Nepal.
Visited Kashmir on leave.

1899 Moved 5th Dragoon Guards to Sialkot. Instituted changes in barracks for comfort of men.
Home on leave.
Ordered by Lord Wolseley on special service to South Africa to raise North-West Frontier Police.
Boer War October 11. Defence of Mafeking.
Published *Aids to Scouting.*

1900 Mafeking relieved—May 17.
Promoted Major-General by the Queen.
Commanded Column against Boers in Transvaal—with Plumer second in command—May to October.

Raised and organised South African Constabulary, 11,000 strong.
Published *Sport in War*.

1901 Home for three months' sick-leave.
Visited King Edward at Balmoral. Received C.B. and Queen's and King's South African War Medals (2).

1902 Boer War ended. S.A.C. took over policing whole country, Transvaal and Orange Free State.
Much travelling, including some long rides, inspecting the different posts.
Conducted Joseph Chamberlain through Transvaal.

1903 Appointed Inspector-General of Cavalry.
Farewell Parades of S.A.C.
Returned home to take up appointment.
Visited German Cavalry School, Hanover.
Visited America—battlefields—West Point—Cavalry Regiments. Also Canada.
Visited Cavalry Schools at Saumur and Vienna.
Spent Christmas at Mentone.

1904 Attended French Cavalry Manoeuvres, Bar-le-Duc.
Started Cavalry School, Netheravon.

1905 Visited Cavalry Schools in Italy, Tor di Quinto and Pinerolo.
Started the *Cavalry Journal*.

1906 Went to South Africa with Duke of Connaught, I.G. Forces.
Inspected Cavalry, South Africa.
Visited Victoria Falls—also East Africa—also Egypt.
Visited Belgian Cavalry, Brussels.

1907 Visited Egypt and Sudan inspecting Cavalry.
Completed term of office as I.G. Cavalry.
Published *Sketches in Mafeking and East Africa*.
Exhibited 126 drawings at Bruton Gallery and bust of John Smith at Royal Academy.
Visited Holland.
Trial Camp of Boy Scouts at Brownsea Island, Dorset.
Promoted Lieut.-General.

1908 Published *Scouting for Boys*.
Appointed to command Northumbrian Territorial Division.
Started *The Scout* newspaper for boys.
Organised Boy Scouts throughout the Empire.

1909 Visited Brazil, Argentine, Chile.
Published *Scouting Games*.
Rally of Boy Scouts at Crystal Palace (11,000) and Scottish Boy Scouts at Glasgow (6,000).
Created K.C.V.O. and K.C.B.

1910 Resigned Territorial Division, March 31.
Retired from Army on to Reserve, May 7, with Reward for Good Service.
Visited Canada and U.S.A. to organise Scouts.
Order of Merit, Chile.
Received LL.D., Edinburgh University.
Visited Paris, St. Petersburg and Moscow (received by Czar) to organise Scouts.
Published *Yarns for Boy Scouts*.

1911 Appointed Colonel 13th Hussars, November 26.
Visited Norway and Sweden for sport and Scouting.
Interviews with King and Crown Prince of Sweden.
Attended King's Coronation. Received Coronation Medal.

1912 Visited Panama, West Indies, U.S.A., Japan, Australia South Africa, New Zealand.
Gave 41 addresses to public on Scouting, 63 speeches.
69 Scout addresses to total of 70,280 people.
Visited Norway.
Knight of St. John of Jerusalem.
Published *Scouts Overseas*.
Met and married Olave St. Clair Soames.
Obtained Royal Charter for Boy Scouts.

1913 With Lady B.-P. visited Algeria, Malta, Naples, etc.
Master of Mercers' Company.
Published *Scouting Games*.
Inspected big Scout Rally at Birmingham, first attended by foreign Scouts.
Freedom of City of Kingston.
Son (Arthur Robert Peter), born October 30.

1914 Raised Boy Scout Endowment Fund (£100,000).
London Boy Scouts inspected by Queen Alexandra on Horse Guards Parade.
Great War. Mobilised Scouts to form guards for rail. ways, etc., and take over Coastguard work.
Mother died, October 13.
Published *Quick Training for War*.

1915 Inspected Boy Scouts on Coastwatching Duty.
Visited the Armies in France as guest of Sir John French, British C.-in-C.
Published *Indian Memories*, also *The Adventures of a Spy*. Addressed six meetings, Liverpool, on behalf of Y.M.C.A.
Daughter (Heather Grace), born June 1.

1916 Visits to British Armies in France.
Girl Guide Conference, Matlock. Lady B.-P. elected Chief Commissioner of Girl Guides.
Inauguration of Wolf Cub Movement.
Published *Young Knights of the Empire*, also *Wolf-Cubs' Handbook* and newspaper.

1917 Conference of Scout Commissioners at Matlock.
Daughter (Betty St. Clair), born April 16.

1918 Boy Scout Conferences, Bournemouth, Edinburgh, Glasgow, Newcastle and London.
Published *Girl Guiding*.
Established Flax-gathering Camps for Boy Scouts.
Queen Alexandra reviewed Girl Guides.
Member of War Museum Committee.
Visited front in France. Visited Scouts in Spain and Portugal.
Armistice, November 11.
Bought Pax Hill, Bentley, Hants.

1919 With Lady B.-P. to Canada and U.S.A. to develop Scouts and Guides.
Published *Aids to Scoutmastership*.
Started Scoutmasters' Training School at Gilwell Park.
Order of Alfonso XII of Spain.

1920 International Jamboree of Boy Scouts, Olympia, London, attended by representatives from all countries.
Elected Chief Scout of the World.
International Scout Bureau started in London.
Orders—Redeemer of Greece, and Christ of Portugal.

1921 With Lady B.-P. to India at invitation of Viceroy (Lord Chelmsford) to organise Scout and Guide Movement. Also visited Scouts and Guides in Burma, Ceylon, Palestine, Egypt. Visited France to see American Camp for Boy Scouts in the devastated area.

Created Baronet.
Published *What Scouts Can Do* and *An Old Wolf's Favourites*.

1922 Visited Belgium, saw Scouts, Cardinal Mercier, and King Albert.
Royal Charter granted to Girl Guides' Association.
Published *Rovering to Success*.
Posse of Welcome to Prince of Wales by 60,000 Scouts at Alexandra Palace.
Received Legion of Honour (Commander).
Addressed International Scout Conference, Paris, and International Education Conference, Geneva.

1923 Awarded G.C.V.O.
With Lady B.-P. visited Canada for International Education Conference. Addressed meetings and saw Scouts and Guides at many main centres.
LL.D., Toronto and McGill Universities.
Returned via U.S.A.
President Old Carthusian Club.
Published new edition of *Pigsticking*.
D.C.L., Oxford University.

1924 Empire Jamboree at Wembley Exhibition, where the Prince of Wales camped with the Scouts.
International Jamboree at Copenhagen.
First World Camp of Girl Guides at Foxlease.

1925 Opening of International Scout Chalet at Kandersteg in the Swiss Alps.
President of the Federation of Rambling Clubs.
Grand Cross of Order of Dannebrog.

1926 With Lady B.-P. visited America as guests of the Boy Scouts of America.
First Rover Scout 'Moot' at Albert Hall, London.
With Lady B.-P. and children visited South Africa, spent seven months there, travelled 8,498 miles inspecting Scouts and Guides and promoting the Movement.
International Scout Conference, Kandersteg.
International Sea Scout Regatta, Antwerp.

1927 Returned from South Africa.
Awarded G.C.M.G.
International Jamboree in Sweden.
Published *Life's Snags*.

1928 Visited Hungary for International Conference of Girl Guides.
Inspected Scouts at Budapest, etc.
Received survivors of original Brownsea Scout Camp (1907) to lunch at Pax Hill.
Visited Scouts in Wales and Irish Free State.
Polish Order of Pologna Restituta.

1929 With Lady B.-P. visited British, French, Spanish and Portuguese Scouts and Guides in the course of a cruise in the *Duchess of Richmond*.
Published *Scouting and Youth Movements*.
Visited France and Belgium.
Received Freedom of Poole and of Blandford.
Jamboree to mark 21st Anniversary of Scout Movement at Arrowe Park, Birkenhead, attended by 56,000 Scouts from 54 countries.
Received from Scouts of the World a motor car, caravan trailer, portrait by David Jagger and cheque.
Order of Phoenix of Greece, Order of White Lion of Czecho-Slovakia, Order of Merit of Hungary.
Created Baron with title 'Baden-Powell of Gilwell'.
Granted Freedom of City of London.

1930 With Lady B.-P. visited West Indies and Bermuda and home via New York, joint banquet, from Boy Scouts and Girl Scouts.
Granted Freedom of Canterbury.
Lady B.-P. elected Chief Guide of the World.

1931 With Lady B.-P. visited Australia, New Zealand, South Africa, addressing meetings and inspecting Scouts and Guides.
Attended International Scouters' Conference at Baden bei Wein, Austria.
Awarded Order of Merit of Austria by President Midlas.
LL.D. of Cambridge University.

1932 With Lady B.-P. attended opening of the International Girl Guide Chalet at Adelboden, Switzerland.
Visited Swiss Scouts' Camp—also that of Dutch Scouts at The Hague.
Awarded Order of Orange of Nassau of Holland.
Awarded Grand Cross of Gedimanas (Lithuania).

Lady B.-P. created Dame Grand Cross of Order of the British Empire.

1933 With Lady B.-P. visited Scouts and Guides in Malta and Gibraltar. Also visited Italy; had interview with Mussolini and audience with the Pope. Saw the Ballilla and their Training Schools, etc.
International Jamboree at Godollo, Hungary.
Awarded Grand Cross of Order of Sword of Sweden.
Awarded Grand Cross of Order of Three Stars of Latvia.
Awarded Red Cross of Estonia.
Visited (with 650 Scouters and Guiders) Scouts and Guides of Holland, Poland, Lithuania, Latvia, Estonia, Finland, Sweden and Norway in S.S. *Calgaric*.
Published *Lessons of the Varsity of Life*.
Received Freedom of Pontefract.

1934 Laid up for five months after serious operation. Visited (with 670 Scouters and Guiders) Scouts and Guides in Malta, Gibraltar, Nice, Algiers, Lisbon, in the S.S. *Adriatic*.
With Lady B.-P. attended Jamboree at Frankston, Melbourne, Australia, visiting *en route* Scouts and Guides of Ceylon, Malaya, Java, Port Darwin, Thursday Island.
Published *Adventures and Accidents*.

1935 Visited New Zealand, South Sea Island, Canada, Newfoundland and the United States, inspecting Scouts and Guides. Visited the President of the U.S. at White House, returning home in S.S. *Majestic*.
Son (Peter) married to Carine Boardman.
Attended World Rover Moot in Sweden.
Left for Kenya, Uganda, Tanganyika, Zanzibar, Rhodesia.
Scout Jamboree at East London, S. Africa.
Published *Scouting Round the World*.

1936 Revisited Mafeking with Lady B.-P. and family.
Returned to England via St. Helena and Ascension I.
Attended Commissioners' Conference at Norwich.
Scout and Guide Dinner of Welcome, London.
Daughter (Betty) married at Bentley (September 24) to Gervas Clay.

Awarded Grand Cordon of Legion of Honour (France).
Visited Scouts and Guides of France (Paris).
Published *Adventuring to Manhood.*

1937 Sailed (January) for India. Scout Jamboree at Delhi.
Spent 80th birthday with 13/18th Hussars, last mounted ceremonial parade of Regiment.
Saw Kadir Cup Competition.
Returned to England. Inspected Scouts on duty at Coronation (Coronation Medal, George VI).
Inspection of Scouts by King and Queen at Windsor.
Awarded Order of Merit.
Visited Holland for International Jamboree at Bloemendaal and International Conference at The Hague.
Awarded Wateler Peace Prize.
Silver Wedding Anniversary Dinner, London.
Published *African Adventures.*
Sailed for Kenya.

1938 Returned to England.
Visited (with 470 Scouters and Guiders) Iceland, Norway, Denmark, Belgium, in S.S. *Orduna.*
Built Paxtu at Nyeri, Kenya.
Published *Birds and Beasts in Africa.*
Returned to Kenya.

1939 Remained in Kenya.
Family Reunion of children and grandchildren at Paxtu, Nyeri.
Published *Paddle Your Own Canoe.*
Exhibited sketches at Officers' Art Society, London, and Kenya Art Exhibition, Nairobi.

1940 Published *More Sketches of Kenya.*
Began *Snaps and Scraps.*
Daughter (Heather) married John King (June 16) at Bentley.

1941 ⊙ January 7. Military Funeral, Nyeri. Memorial Service, Westminster Abbey, January 27.
Memorial services throughout world during January.